BARRIO PRINCESS
GROWING UP IN TEXAS

The author's second grade photograph, showing what her mother called "Shirley Temple curls"

BARRIO PRINCESS

GROWING UP IN TEXAS

By Consuelo Samarripa

Parkhurst Brothers Publishers
MARION, MICHIGAN

www.parkhurstbrothers.com

Parkhurst Brothers books are distributed to the trade through the Chicago Distribution Center, and may be ordered through Ingram Book Company, Baker & Taylor, Follett Library Resources and other book industry wholesalers. To order from Chicago Distribution Center, phone 800-621-2736 or send a fax to 800-621-8476. Copies of this and other Parkhurst Brothers Publishers titles are available to organizations and corporations for purchase in quantity by contacting Special Sales Department at our home office location, listed on our website. Manuscript submission guidelines for this publishing company are available at our website.

Printed in the United States of America
First Edition, 2014
2014 2015 2016 2017 2018 2019 2020
12 11 10 9 8 7 6 5 4 3 2

Library of Congress Cataloging-in-Publication Data

Samarripa, Consuelo, 1947-
    Barrio princess : growing up in Texas / Consuelo Samarripa. -- First edition.
        pages cm
    Summary: "The personal stories of a Mexican-American born into the San Antonio Barrio in the late 1940s, including family stories, cultural tradition stories, learning English by total immersion, socialization as a minority, education, and stories of her mother as a single parent, and women's stories from a minority point of view"-- Provided by publisher.
    Summary: "A woman's experience of growing up speaking Spanish when there was no provision for non-English speakers in public schools in America, including her social, educational, worklife and family challenges as she became a contributing member of a society that was often not receptive to her gender, color or contrbutions"-- Provided by publisher.
    ISBN 978-1-62491-027-2 (paperback) -- ISBN 978-1-62491-029-6 (hardback) -- ISBN 978-1-62491-028-9 (ebk)
    1. Samarripa, Consuelo, 1947- 2. Mexican American women--Texas--San Antonio--Biography. 3. Mexican Americans--Texas--San Antonio--Social conditions. 4. Mexican Americans--Texas--San Antonio--Social life and customs. 5. San Antonio (Tex.)--Social conditions--20th century. I. Title.
    F394.S2119M51743 2014
    305.48'868720730764092--dc23
    [B]
                                    2014016048

This book is printed on archival-quality paper that meets requirements of the American National Standard for Information Sciences, Permanence of Paper, Printed Library Materials, ANSI Z39.48-1984.

Cover photo by	Montez-Barron, Samarripa family archives
Cover design:	Linda Parkhurst PhD
Page design:	Linda Parkhurst PhD
Proofreaders:	Bill and Barbara Paddack
Acquired for Parkhurst Brothers Publishers	
And edited by:	Ted Parkhurst
072014	

This book is dedicated to

Andrew Jr., Karen and Benjamin
Lauren, Zachary, Veronica, Noah, Jacob,
Gabriel, Mia and Nathaniel

Con todo el amor de "Mamacita"

Acknowledgements

Storytellers believe a story is a gift. Some storytellers also believe a person is remembered and kept alive by the re-telling of their story.

This book goes out in remembrance of my ancestors, including my beloved maternal grandmother, Basilia Montez Barron. It also goes to give loving thanks to my mother, Guadalupe Barron McNeir. When she didn't have the answers for me, she urged me to find the answers the best way I could. I am grateful to my uncles, aunts and cousins who inspired some of these stories for family is the foundation of my Mexican-American cultural family life and heritage.

A big heartfelt appreciation goes to my many cousins who confirmed or assisted my memory of the chronological order of some family events. My cousins who lived up and down Ruiz Street at one time or the other were especially helpful. Each one is a continuing blessing, and each recalling of family events is deeply appreciated.

School days were made memorable by my Killeen High School class of 1966 friends. You accepted, befriended and inspired me to be playful, learn and write. I appreciate you all, and send a sincere thanks for the memories.

Friends from Ludwigsburg American High School in Germany, Barb Park Gillaspie, Pat Byrd Robinson and Leandra Ash Steinberg: you have been there bridging me through discouraging times. Thank you for helping me return to writing.

A special recognition with a literary rose goes to the school and college educators who influenced and inspired me: Mrs. Vinnie Craig, who taught me spelling; Mrs. Lona Riemenshneider, for turning on the light of learning and reading for pleasure; and Miss Susie Jorgenson, for encouraging my creative traits in art and writing. Finally, my sincere gratitude is extended to Dr. Donna Ingham for challenging me to be a writer with joyful certitude, for long hours listening and giving feedback. Thank you for mentoring me through the years. Donna, it has been a joy to see our lives come full circle through the power of storytelling. Who knew?

Mil gracias, to Lydia Salazar for her assistance in editing the Spanish, you are so remarkable.

Appreciative acknowledgements go to Lisa Youngblood and the Harker Heights Library staff for their untiring support and for providing opportunities for me to use a library computer when my own personal computer was on the blitz while writing this book.

Very special hugs, admiration, adoring recognition and love go to my children and grandchildren for being patient listeners and for giving me feedback on my stories through the years.

Finally, a distinct appreciative gratefulness goes to Ted Parkhurst for his encouragement, and for his extraordinary patience while working with me. Ted, thank you for virtually holding my hand and for committed guidance on this journey to publish with Parkhurst Brothers.

To all of you "*que dios les dé más de lo que me han dado*," may God give you more than you have given me.

Muchas gracias.

Consuelo Samarripa
Harker Heights, Texas
January 2014

The author's first grade photograph—the year she began to learn English

Table of Contents

The author, age 5, at Woodland Park, San Antonio, Texas. The woman silhouetted in the background may be her mother.

I

La Curandera Del Barrio

The Neighborhood Faith Healer, the Folk Healer

Los Aztecas, the Aztecs, had a medical belief system in place long before the Anglos and Spaniards came to the southwestern parts of the United States. This Native American medical belief system was practiced by the male *curanderos* or the female *curanderas*. These *curanderos y curanderas* were our folk healers, our faith healers. They practiced at different levels from regions to our neighborhoods, *en los barrios*. The most famous regional *curandero* in Texas was named *Don Pedrito Jaramillo*, the healer of *Rancho de Los Olmos*, from the Ranch of the Elm Trees. A shrine stands near Falfurrias, Texas, in loving memory of *Don Pedrito*.

Curanderos y curanderas practiced healing in our Mexican-Indian culture. There were never any certifications, diplomas or such documents of expertise and knowledge. Mostly, they tried to remedy physical, spiritual and sometimes psychological ailments or illnesses with herbal teas. These folk healers provided cures for the indigenous people native to Texas. They did healings with some degree of success. The *curandera* of our Westside *barrio* in San Antonio was named *Doña Basilia*. One of her favorite herbs was sage; she even had a Texas sage bush growing in her yard. Of course, her sage bush had Mexican purple blossoms. She healed aches, sprains and strains with her hand massages and oils. Other times she cured ailments with herbal teas.

Once she taught me to brew a tea to treat my cold. She told me to break a few fresh sprigs from her sage bush in her yard. After a gentle rinse in water, the sage leaves were stripped until there were enough to fill a small amount in the palm of my cupped hand. The sage bush leaves were added to boiling water to brew. The exact amount of water to boil was measured only by the ring around the small sauce pan she used for teas. Tea pots were not in her vocabulary and thus not in her kitchen inventory. Finally, she specifically said to use honey to sweeten the tea. The tea was comforting and its steamy fragrance refreshing in spite of the cold.

It was the practice of our family and neighborhood friends to first seek help from a *curandera* before a doctor. *La jente del barrio en la calle Ruiz*, the people living along Ruiz Street, went to *Doña Basilia* for whatever ailed them. She was wise with her Native American remedies. *Unos dicien que podía hacer milagros con sus manos y remedios*, Once, I heard a lady say she performed miracles with her healing hands and her remedies.

Doña Basilia's healings and prayer chants were always done with good intentions for her people.

She was also the midwife of the neighborhood. *La partera del barrio* is what we called her in Spanish. She and her sister-in-law Blanca were *parteras*, mid-wives. *Doña Basilia* helped bring many *barrio* children into this world, including several of my cousins. Her most memorable delivery was delivering me, I guess because it *was* me. Her most noted delivery was a set of twin boys. As adults, the twins paid their respects and accompanied *Doña Basilia's* family when she passed away.

In old traditional Mexican lore, a person can make someone ill just by staring intensively. Regardless of the intent, it can be perceived as imparting the evil eye or a curse. Our Native American belief is that some people possess a stronger spiritual good or bad power, that the stronger-willed person can deplete the spirit of the weaker soul. A common Mexican belief is if a person admires an object worn or possessed by another, the admirer must touch the admired object. Although there is no *mal* intent, the practice in touching the object is a preventive measure to deter any ill will that may be perceived. Often, bad luck or envy is associated with the evil eye *malaise* too.

Sometimes when a baby cries uncontrollably or has unexplained weight loss, even fever, aches, pains, or physical weaknesses, these are classic symptoms of *"mal ojo."* Other signs of *mal* intent are bad business or perhaps unexplained accidents.

These indigenous views may seem silly; nevertheless, these folk beliefs and lore are still practiced today in Mexican communities, as in other world cultures.

Aunt Rosalinda lived several blocks away. In the summer of 1954, she gave birth to my little cousin Alejandro. A month before his first birthday Alejandro was afflicted with an ailment that weakened his right leg. My aunt asked *Doña Basilia* to perform a sweeping. In Spanish, we called the practice *barrer,* to sweep. She swept him to cure the affliction of his leg, *ella barrió a Alejandro para curar la aflicción de la pierna de Alejandro.*

Contrary to foreign thinking, a house broom was not used to do the curing sweep. Actually, the sweeping was done using a whole raw egg in the shell to extract the bad powers, *mal ojo*, from the body. *Doña Basilia* rubbed the afflicted leg many times as she prayed. She brushed and rubbed the whole egg over his body while chanting prayers. Next, she cracked the egg open and carefully dropped it into a glass that had been partially filled with water. For this process, *Doña Basilia* did not require a special container like a scientific beaker. *Doña Basilia* simply used an old empty jelly glass. She placed the glass with its new contents under little Alejandro's bed. The following morning, *Doña Basilia* returned to assess Alejandro's ailment by evaluating the contents of the glass from under his bed. Only *Doña Basilia* knew what she was looking for. The "patient" usually felt better the day after the sweeping. However, there was no improvement in little Alejandro's leg over the next several days. *Doña Basilia* was very wise and proud, yet her pride never interfered with a client's best interest.

Doña Basilia told my aunt little Alejandro needed to be evaluated by a medical doctor. Aunt Rosalinda and Uncle Alejandro, Sr., took my young cousin to the doctor. They learned Alejandro had poliomyelitis. He was a victim of the 1955 polio epidemic like millions of other babies of that time. He was spared the "iron lung" treatment that was used for the more serious polio cases. Instead, his leg was restrained with a brace. It saddened us to see his tiny leg in a brace at such a young age.

One day, *Doña Basilia* went to my aunt's house with a

new remedy. *Doña Basilia* opened a small colorful pumpkin orange box bearing the brand McLean's. She pulled out a brown beer bottle of dark oil. The scent of turpentine identified the base of the oil used for muscle aches and pains. It was also good for joint pain. *Doña Basilia* frequently used this oil liniment that she simply called "*volcanico*," in her healings.

I had never observed the "*volcanico*" cure *this* way before. *Doña Basilia* unbuckled the restraining leather straps from the metal leg brace that Alejandro wore. When she opened the brown bottle, a potent turpentine scent saturated the room with hope. The scent lingered in my memories with the healing attempts for Alejandro for many years, just as the scent lingered in the room at that moment.

The brown oil drops fell into the cupped palm of *Doña Basilia's* hand, until she held a small dark brown puddle. The *mestizo* hands gently came together as if to avoid spilling the potential cure. She rubbed the two hands together as if in prayer. Then the hopeful cure began.

Gently, she massaged little Alejandro's foot and leg muscle with the *volcanico* as she softly chanted her prayers. The room was filled with the aroma of the *volcanico* and murmurs of hopeful prayers from both the *curandera* and loved ones wringing their hands as they stood at the foot of the bed.

She placed one hand under little Alejandro's foot and the other hand under his lower leg muscle. *Doña Basilia* started by lifting the foot to balance it and then lifting the lower leg in such a way his leg was in a "Z" position. She held Alejandro's leg so it was offset, yet parallel with his body. She slid her hand to rest at the back of his knee, from where she would guide the exercise. Then, she gently stretched his afflicted leg's knee toward my cousin's chest. All the while, she still maintained the lower leg in a "Z" position. His knee naturally stretched folding toward his chest, in a collapsed "Z" position. *Doña Basilia* softly whispered her prayers. She repeated the muscle stretching exercise for a half hour. Finally, *Doña Basilia* wrapped towels around the leg before letting it rest to absorb the "cure" with the warmth of the *volcanico*. She told my aunt to replace the polio brace on Alejandro after a while. *Doña Basilia* returned and repeated this process, or therapy, for many days. Sadly, there was no immediate change in his condition, no evident cure for my cousin, Alejandro.

Although none of us realized it at the time and some may not realize it to this day, little Alejandro was fighting a heroic battle. It was his battle, *era su batalla*. Sometimes, when a warrior marches into battle against a feared enemy, he is wounded. Alejandro fought the battle against a feared and mysterious enemy that threatened each of us. In his case – the enemy was polio. His wounded knee reminded us we were spared. We were spared from polio because our families diligently made certain we got our polio vaccines. We lined up in the school cafeteria where a sugar cube was placed on our outstretched tongues by a nurse dressed entirely in white. Later, it was explained to us that a dosage of the Salk polio vaccine had been soaked into the sugar cube we had eaten. We were relieved to hear that, rather than facing a dreaded syringe, we had been "treated" with a cube of sugar. The dosage tasted like the spoonful of sugar my grandmother gave us as a remedy to cure immediate fears and to stop tears. Funny, both of the sweet dosages had the similar effects.

Without Alejandro's battle so close to our homes,

our families would never have been aware of the crippling, sometimes deadly outcome from the polio epidemic of 1955. He was our hero.

Years later, I saw a movie in which a nurse practiced the same method *Doña Basilia* had used as therapy on a polio victim. In the movie, the nurse used a lotion and exercised the patient's leg, just the way I had seen *Doña Basilia* practice on little Alejandro. According to the movie, Sister Elizabeth Kenny, an Australian nurse, had introduced the technique, which was called the Sister Kenny polio therapy or treatment. It was controversial at the outset. But, Sister Kenny passionately believed instead of immobilizing the muscles, the muscles needed to be "retrained." Sister Kenny's "retraining" method was based on massaging and exercising the muscle to rehabilitate the leg, rather than restricting it. She would do the therapy, then wrap the afflicted area with warm cloths. I was shocked how the Kenny treatment was like the *curandera's* practice, except *Doña Basilia's* method used the *volcanico* as the heat source.

Doña Basilia was as ethical as any medical doctor. She was wise enough to realize what she could cure and what she could not.

Besides physical ailments, she tried to cure our undisciplined ways or manners by guiding us with wise sayings and proverbs. The proverbs – we called them *dichos* – taught us many life lessons. When she had company, the *dicho* I heard most often became the one I remembered longest. Sometimes, as a child, I interrupted her guests' conversations abruptly. To correct my bad manners, she would say, *"En boca cerrada, no entran moscas,"* when a mouth is closed, flies cannot enter.

Doña Basilia's gentle admonition has rescued me from eating many flies over the years.

Sometimes parents in the neighborhood sent a child to *Doña Basilia.* She was forewarned when a child was coming to her house for some much-needed "counseling." A good listener, *Doña Basilia* sat quietly for a time as the child in need of guidance whined or complained about the unfairness of life. Then, *Doña Basilia* suggested a resolution or perhaps another way to think about the child's troubles. Usually, she was able to guide him or her into doing the right thing. Sometimes, the advice was taken and sometimes not. Lovingly and persistently, *Doña Basilia* molded us with the *dichos* she kept in her memory bank. She was ready with a *dicho* when the time warranted. *Doña Basilia* was like a walking "dicho-nary."

I was still a teenager when I personally experienced *Doña Basilia's* healing from *susto.* In our Mexican-American culture, an affliction of *susto* always meant a visit to the *curandera.* My summer vacations were spent at *Doña Basilia's* home. My first summer as a high school graduate was no different. Usually, my weight was of no concern to me, but as that summer began, I had lost a lot of weight and was anemic.

Anemia was an intermittent problem for me from a very young age. It was an unforgettable experience for me. One day, I was told to open my mouth for a spoon so large, I was sure the Titanic could have sunk from sight in it! The dreaded spoon was brimming with a liquid vitamin mixture that smelled like dead worms scraped up from the edge of the street (or what my childish brain imagined dead worms might taste like if they were on the healthy food chart). Another day, I gagged down a dose from a tubular dropper filled with the odiferous golden gooey liquid vitamins. Every morning, being the child that I was, I whined like an injured cat.

"*Sabe como gusanos!*" I proclaimed, "It tasted like worms" every morning!

Later, when I was a teenager, my unexplained weight loss was a concern to my mother. I overheard my mother discuss her concern about my health with other well-meaning women who in all their well-meaning diagnoses suspected, perhaps "it might be a tapeworm." Ha! That word was a new one in my vocabulary: tapeworm! But, I was not surprised! I told my mother those liquid vitamins tasted like worms and now they had come back to haunt me!

However, *Doña Basilia* actually suspected it was *susto*. *Susto* means fright, and may, in a certified medical world, suggest anxiety or panic. This was a new malaise to me or at least I thought it was. Perhaps I had not said it out loud. I guess it did worry me and perhaps made me fearful and anxious about what to do with my life.

College was not in my future as it was for some of my friends, especially since going to college did not follow the normal, publicly funded education process like elementary, junior high and high school did. But I wanted to go to college badly. I just thought it was a good idea. The prospect of my future as a late-teens high school graduate was frightening. Perhaps, the sleepless nights and lack of appetite was indeed triggered by *susto*. I was faced with mixed feelings and reservations about the diagnosis along with the joined beliefs from my somewhat scientific mind and my Mexican-American cultural heritage. But I could justify the two.

I conceded and submitted my body and soul to our

neighborhood *curandera*. *Doña Basilia* told me the healing would take place just before I went to sleep for the night. It just so happened I was staying with her that summer, so it was convenient. That night she brewed *té de manzanilla*, sweet yet earthy Mexican chamomile tea. She used the flaxen-colored tea leaves, which were stored in a small brown paper bag. As usual, she used her sauce pan to make the brew. She poured the herbal tea into a white enamel mug decorated with a single bouquet of blue flowers. It was from Mexico and my favorite mug to use on visits to her home. She stirred the herbal tea and sweetened it with a spoonful of beehive honey, *miel de una colmena*. I heard her rolling up the paper bag of remaining sweet scented tea leaves as I blew into the steamy mug. She saved the leaves for another healing at another time. I stared at the tea in the cup. The kitchen light bulb in the ceiling appeared as if it were floating upon the tea itself. I looked up to the primitive light fixture – a light socket, a light bulb and a dangling string. So primitive yet heartwarming, it was a sure sign of home. I remembered the Mexican hospitality saying, "*mi casa, su casa,*" such comforting hospitality to offer one's home as the visitor's home.

Her kitchen was where her family gathered during the holidays, where she and her *comadres* made annual Christmas tamales, where she served tamales to soldiers without passes to go home for the holidays and where many a counseling of one kind or another happened. All at the kitchen table under the primitive lighting.

And then she came to sit across the kitchen table from me where she had full view of me and her kitchen. We chatted a bit while I sipped the comforting brew but it was her presence that I found most comforting.

She finally escorted me to my bed for the night. The room had statues of the Virgin Mary, a cross with the crucified Jesus, three votive candles – all her Catholic religious artifacts – atop a doily. It was her altar where she kneeled and prayed at night, or in the day when she had her own worries. Earlier, she had gathered enough roses from her yard to fill a mason jar that was now placed in the middle of the altar. It was customary for her to do just that when her roses were in bloom. The rose scent reassured me of her love. The candles flickering at her altar shed the only light in the room. That dancing candlelight comforted me as peacefully then as holy day candlelight does now.

Later, I learned there were two types of *susto*. There is *pasado*, which is fright "from or in the past" that has been left untreated, while *liviano* is a "more recently triggered" fright. Surely my *susto* was *liviano*.

She asked me to lie on the bed, *como Christo en la cruz*. I understood she meant for me to rest "like Christ on the cross." I crossed my feet quite naturally. However, it was uncomfortable extending my arms out from the small bed. So I folded them in, like chicken wings, which was more fitting since I was a little scared and feeling chicken with the healing process. *Doña Basilia* knew me too well. She adjusted my arms out so my body resembled Christ on the cross just as she had directed. Then, she walked to her altar to get her bottle of holy water. She poured a little holy water in her plump *mestizo* hand, as she made the sign of the cross to bless herself and in our Catholic way, she whispered, "*En el nombre del Padre, el Hijo y el Espíritu Santo, Amen.*" Then in sacred succession, she tapped her forehead, her mid-chest, her left shoulder, her right shoulder and finally her lips. It was the practice we used to bless ourselves and to chant, "In the name of the Father, the Son and the Holy Spirit, Amen," as we entered the church. We blessed ourselves this way just before any prayers, as we walked or drove past a Catholic Church, as a hearse or dead body passed by us, upon the death of a person or a pet, upon arrival on a visit to a gravesite and when we were fearful or uncertain.

She dribbled more holy water in her hands and blessed me the same way she had done with herself; another dribble blessed the rest of my body. All the while, she was praying. Occasionally, she inhaled deeply and exhaled a sigh, which was not part of the process but seemed to confirm the burden of her advanced age.

Next, she began the sweeping. This time she used a small "brush" of sagebrush twigs with leaves, sweeping over my body while she intoned low prayers and chants. The sweeping tickled me and I giggled. Even though it had been more than a decade since I had moved away from the old ways, I was trying to take this seriously, an effort complicated by the tickling.

"*No te rías*." She meant for me to "stop laughing." She said this in a somber and firm manner, the same somber and firm manner as the look she gave me.

"*Pero me hace cosquillas*." I explained to her the sagebrush twigs were "tickling me." All at once I realized that while I was pleading like a child, I was also trying to restrain my nervous young woman giggles.

"*No te rías*," She insisted that I "stop laughing." She swept more, sparing no chance for *susto* to endure.

My thoughts were realigned to respect my beloved elder's loving ways to heal.

"*¡Cony, vente! ¡Cony, vente! ¡No te quedes!*" She called me "Cony," her nickname for me. Lovingly, she was calling to me to, "Come on, come on and do not stay behind."

"*¿A dónde vamos, Nana?*" In my confusion I asked her, "Where are we going, Nana?" This was not a respectful way to respond. Unaware of her procedure, I wanted to know where we were going.

"*Shhhhh!*" She insisted on serenity.

In the candlelight, there was a little frustration on her face. She continued.

"*Sólo responde así. ¡Ay voy!*"

She guided me by telling me how to respond. My response was to say "I'm coming." Her face glowed with its endearing patience yet there was no reassuring smile. Her eyes met mine and certainly she knew I was puzzled about what was happening, where was I supposed to be going? Was I supposed to remove myself from the affliction and all negative airs? I was trying to keep the faith of her healing abilities. But then, she already knew I had faith, she had repeatedly ingrained in me the importance of keeping the faith. It was I who doubted myself and my faith. I closed my eyes and concentrated, trying to get a sense of the healing throughout my body.

Then again, this time she said.

"*¡Cony, vente! No te quedes! ¡Cony, vente! ¡No te quedes!*"

"*¡Ay voy! ¡Ay voy!*" I guessed I was supposed to repeat my phrases too.

She had repeated the process perhaps for extra measure.

I didn't know how many more times we were going to do this. If I was not afflicted with anxiety before now, I was surely on my way to it as we continued. Then, as she swept my body one last time with the sagebrush twigs, whispering her prayers over my body, a sense of relief settled within me. I sensed she was also achieving a relief of the acceptance of the cure.

"Ya," she said tenderly. The healing completed, she made the sign of the cross on my forehead with her plump thumb just as she had done when I was little and said, "*Ahora, mijita a dormir. Que Dios te guarde,*" now, it is time to sleep. She was saying, may God protect and guard you.

My giggling had stopped. My faith and confidence had been restored. Everything would be all right. The faith healer blessed me. She knew what she could cure and what she could not. She was our wisest elder, *Doña Basilia, la curandera del barrio*, the neighborhood folk healer, the faith healer.

There, in the same room, the room where she helped bring me into this world, I slipped into a restful sleep among the fragrance of roses and the tranquil glow of candlelight.

II

Delphiniums, Delphiniums, Delphiniums

En lo fresco del día, in the freshness of the day, *mi abuelita* liked making *tortillas,* ironing, washing clothes, sewing and doing her daily household chores. She especially enjoyed watering the flower beds in the early morning, as the day was breaking.

I awoke as the sky's gray light waited for the sun to rise above the barrio rooftops. It was so unusually early. Somehow, the cotton sheet had already been thrown off, so it was so easy for me to roll over and slide down from the bed. My bare feet landed gently yet firmly on the hardwood floor. My soft white cotton nightgown hung down to the floor barely draping across my Texas tanned toes.

What *Abuelita* and I called my nightgown was actually a simple old T-shirt my uncle had worn until it felt soft to the touch. From time to time, *Abuelita* sorted articles of clothing into piles for re-use. There was a quilting patches pile and the dusting and rag mop pile. Select articles of clothing to be recycled for use by different family members made up a third pile. I called it the *todavía sirve* pile because she mumbled those words when she tossed an article of clothing into the "it still serves a purpose" pile. The supple T-shirt came from her *todavía sirve* pile. It served another purpose when it became my soft nightgown.

It was in the air; there was something strange about that morning. The clanging of pots and pans, the music from the Zenith radio, and the morning smells of tortilla griddles warming up and the cooking of tortillas that often arose from the kitchen had not awakened me as usual. But there was a slight aroma of the morning coffee in *Abuelita's* house. It only took a few steps to persuade my sleepy body to shuffle its way to the kitchen. But, my grandmother was not there. She was rarely out of her kitchen in the early morning. Even in my early childhood reasoning, it was easy to conclude that probably she was outside on the front porch. My body spun around making my nightgown twirl. I loved making my dresses and gowns twirl. I spun myself silly until I remembered I was on a mission. I walked through a small bedroom, which was once a small dining room, then into the living room and finally to the front door.

The front screen door hung from a plain door frame. Across the lower half of the door, three slats ran across the door, holding the screen in place.

The door was worn from *Abuelita's* open door policy. I threw a braid, quite naturally, over each of my shoulders. This allowed me to see better when I searched for my *abuelita*. My small hands grasped one of the screen door's stabilizing slats. The clasp of my small fingers and thumb froze on the screen door slat to help me keep my balance else I might have fallen through the unlatched door. My neck swayed to duck my head under the blinding slats to allow me a better peek outside. Just like my Aunt Carlotita's Felix the Cat clock, my eyes shifted slowly from side to side searching for *Abuelita* through the screen. She was not sitting with a cup of coffee on her powdery white porch glider as she sometimes did in the early morning. If she was somewhere in the front yard, I could not see her from my front door view.

Releasing my grasp from the door slat to lightly push the screen door open, I stepped out to hunt for my *abuelita*. My bare feet were chilled by the cool front porch concrete. The chill against the soles of my feet immediately propped my feet up on their toes – just like a ballerina. Slowly, I tiptoed to the opposite edge of the porch. There, my feet flattened again into a firm stance. My toes curled on the porch's edge like a skin-clad fringe of bone. It was something I often did at the edge of the porch at any given time – just one of my youthful quirks like mimicking Felix the Cat's clock eyes. I spotted her, studied her for a moment from the porch, the same porch I saw built into a concrete form from an old rotting wooden porch. That all happened about the same time the royal blue house address plaque, shaped like the Alamo, was hung next to her front door. I had studied it so many times from the front porch glider. Her name, Basilia M. Barron, appeared in small Arial font. Her name was above the house numbers, with "Ruiz Street" at the sign's base.

Her house originally had wooden slats, which were "upgraded" to white asbestos siding. The white asbestos siding was completed after her new kitchen and bathroom were added. The kitchen was our favorite place in her house. The remodeling was done a few years before the concrete sidewalk, steps and porch (from which I now watched my *abuelita*) were added.

Abuelita was kneeling on a small stack of folded newspapers at her flower garden's edge. A slightly bigger pile of folded newspapers was at her side ready to serve as her next knee pad.

Just three little hops down the porch steps and I was at ground level, just like she was. I scampered across the yard to reach her at the flower bed. Just two steps into my dash, I felt the morning dew droplets on the St. Augustine grass dampen the soles of my feet. The heels of my feet pulled up once again and I tiptoed to my grandmother. Laying my head on her back, I wrapped my skinny arms around her rotund grandmother's body. Baptized in her warmth, I absorbed her love. The morning greetings had begun.

"*Buenos días, Abuelita.*" Every morning I said, "Good morning, *Abuelita.*"

"*Buenos días. ¿Y cómo está mi reina hoy?*" – Good morning. And how is my queen today? I heard those unforgettable words so often as part of our morning greetings. The words were always so endearing, always spoken in Spanish.

"*Bien.*" I let her know her queen was "well." It was a time when a princess lived in a fairy tale book and "the queen" lived in *Abuelita's* house!

Abuelita was kneeling on a past issue of the *San Antonio Light*. It was called "Da Light" in her house. Although she could not read or write English, she subscribed to it to see the pictures, department store sale advertisements and the comics.

"Da Light" was delivered every afternoon and on Sunday mornings when the comics appeared in impressive color. She also subscribed to the *San Antonio Express* for a while. It was the newspaper my cousin, Juan Manuel, who we called Johnny, delivered on his bicycle paper route. Only she knew why she subscribed to the *Express.*

I don't recall which newspaper carried the comic strip *Henry,* but I remember she liked to "read" *Henry,* and I did too. *Henry* was a practical comic strip for us to follow since we didn't know how to read English. I didn't know how to read *at all. Henry* was a small bald boy character who often acted out the comic strip story without text. *Abuelita* and I wrinkled our foreheads as we figured out the plot and improvised a story line with words of our own. As my grandmother prepared supper – pans and pots jingling and burping on the stovetop, I opened the newspaper comics section flat on the kitchen's floor and sprawled on my belly to browse.

Sometimes she asked about *Henry* as she cooked, "¿Y qué hace Henry hoy?" – ... and what is *Henry* doing today? She wanted me to tell her my interpretation of *Henry's* actions while she was cooking. Wiping her hands on a muslin apron, she listened while I improvised. Sometimes she laughed out loud as she lifted a wooden spoon to sample one of the supper pans. I wasn't sure what she was laughing about. But her laughter made me laugh and giggle along with her. So *Henry* was part of our common daily humor. That was a good enough reason for her to subscribe to the newspapers, too.

She had no questions about *Henry* that morning.

Instead, I had questions about what she was doing. Usually we did the weeding in the cool evening shadows rather than in the morning.

"*¿Qué hace?*" I asked her – what are you doing?

"*Estoy quitando las malas hierbas para que las plantas puedan crecer.*" She explained that she was removing the weeds so plants could grow. She further explained to always remove bad things that keep other things from growing. Even though I wasn't quite sure, I thought I understood what she meant. I gave her my response.

"Okay." *Okay* was one of those words people understood easily in any language.

Most of the neighbors proudly grew St. Augustine in their front yards. *Las señoras vecinas,* the neighborhood ladies took pride in talking about and watering their St. Augustine grass. It was strange or may have seemed strange to most people, but *Abuelita* taught me the difference between St. Augustine, Bermuda and Johnson grass at a very young age. St. Augustine grass merged with Bermuda grass along one side of *Abuelita's* house. As for Johnson grass, it grew near the very back close to the easement of my grandmother's backyard. She had taught me how to pull, transplant, save to root, and train St. Augustine runners. We pulled the different Bermuda runners from the flower beds and trashed them with the Johnson grass. Sorting out the different grasses was part of the weeding process we did as part of her gardening. It was like sorting clothes.

She continued with the task at hand. She pulled on the Bermuda grass runners that had infiltrated her flourishing flower bed. In spite of the cool morning, perspiration beads dotted her grandmotherly face. Her graying hair appeared moist, too.

She sighed as whispers of prayers came from her lips. *Abuelita* had taught me to always say a prayer when I planted flower seeds or transplanted a potted plant. She had never mentioned anything about praying when pulling weeds. Maybe she was praying they would never come back!

Abuelita was known to pray for others. She prayed for those who were ill, those who were in trouble or at war; she prayed in the morning, during the day or at night, whenever a prayer was needed. She whispered prayers when she had her own worries, too. Sometimes, she prayed with her rosary beads, other times she prayed straight from her heart and soul straight to *Diosito*, our loving God.

I thought I heard her sob. Was she crying? Something was seriously on her mind – and so early in the day! She prayed softly and yanked hard on a Bermuda grass runner. She turned and at the same time she raised her arm to wipe the perspiration from her forehead onto her dress sleeve. Maybe it was tears? Afterward, she grabbed a small fresh stack of "Da Light" and *Express* newspaper mix. It occurred to me *Henry* was somewhere in that mess of newspapers. But *Henry* was not on her mind. She put the newspapers down next to her and transferred her knees, body and all upon fresh padding. She returned to whispered prayers and hearty yanks on weeds. She spared no unwanted weeds, *las hierbas,* the weeds robbed nutrients and moisture from her beloved flowers. *Pobrecitas florisitas,* the poor little flowers.

It was clear that whatever was on her mind would remain unspoken. I was curious, but it was not my place to ask. Suddenly there was one unexpected clue. She had given a quick yank on an unwelcomed weed when the word *"gente"* splattered from her lips with a shower of perspiration, which dripped from her furrowed forehead. My eyes searched her face for more clues. I was very interested in what she might say next, so I waited. There were no other clues, no other words slipping or dropping from her low whispers. Thoughts raced through my young reasoning mind and its rumor bank. What people, *¿qué gente?* I asked myself. I wanted to ask her but it was already ingrained in my mind not to pry in adult matters. It was ingrained because I was often a curious child. Was it people like our relatives? Or people who were not related? What people?

To give her back a quick rest, she raised her upper body and rested on the backs of her legs. With a flick of her wrists, she threw a graying braid over each shoulder. Then she leaned forward to concentrate on more weeds. Her braids rested on her back.

I grabbed some padding and placed my bony knees upon the newspapers. I decided to help her with the weeding. Mimicking her, I threw *my* braids backward to rest on *my* back. Like *Abuelita*, like little queen! I learned to do many things by working alongside her.

Occasionally, she would pause and turn to look at me, then smile lovingly for a moment before returning to her work. It was so easy to return a loving smile back to her – so, so easy. As she returned to weeding, just beyond her profile, the delphiniums caught my eye.

The beautiful blue delphiniums were growing tall on their spikes. *Abuelita* had wrapped a thin white string around and around some sticks to keep the delphiniums healthy, strong and tall. She had them corralled in a showy stall. Some of the sweet peas had climbed onto the unwashed fence and were blooming while the cool green tendrils of other sweet peas were just learning to crawl their way up the fence. Yet other sweet pea vining ringlets hung in midair seeking their way to the delphinium spikes. *Abuelita* trained those away from the delphiniums.

My eyes wandered ahead to the lovely roses in their own separate flower bed. Some of her roses, with their colorful fragrant blooms, were as wide as my grandmother's plump hands. Later she would cut several of the largest blooms to make a bouquet for her religious altar.

But my eyes and thoughts danced back to the delphiniums. I was still in awe of the fine delphiniums. I used my preschooler skills to count them: delphiniums, delphiniums, delphiniums, so many delphiniums. So many beautiful blue shades of delicate flowers clustered on one stem! There were delphiniums, delphiniums, delphiniums, everywhere. They added such peacefulness and graciousness to my grandmother's flower garden.

Many years later, I learned delphiniums and sweet peas were blooming elements of an English garden. I wondered if *Abuelita* knew that. Delphiniums are hard to grow, and require great care and maintenance. It takes a pretty patient gardener to grow them in Texas. Delphiniums require moist, well-drained soil, rarely found in a hot city like San Antonio.

I gathered thoughts of how plants are like people. That's where my thoughts went when I heard *Abuelita* mention *gente*. Maybe she was comparing the two or maybe not. I was learning from our gardening together and did not realize it.

But I did many years later. While bad things can creep into plants' and people's lives, the bad things need to be removed or nipped away to have better growth. Sometimes plants, like people, have to be corralled in their ways to help them grow big, tall, healthy and strong. Plants, like people, may not be native to their environment, but with dedicated care they can bloom beautifully where they are planted.

I never learned what was troubling my grandmother that morning. Whatever it was, she found peace – and perhaps also grace – by clipping and pulling the weeds among her many shades of blue delphiniums. I worried less about her and her worries when I saw the delphiniums. Like people, sometimes plants can bring peace and grace just by their presence. I found a bit of peace myself that morning, just being in the midst of delphiniums, delphiniums, delphiniums – so many peaceful delphiniums.

III

El Milagro en la Calle Ruiz
The Miracle Along Ruiz Street

Everyone knew *Doña* Basilia Barron was the *curandera* of our neighborhood, as well as a wise elder. Most of our relatives lived somewhere in our neighborhood along Ruiz Street at one time or another. They lived either on the west side of Ira Odgen Elementary or the east side. From Ogden, my grandmother's house was halfway down the block on Ruiz on the west side, halfway between Ogden and Mrs. Morgen's store.

I awoke to the sound of clanging pots and pans. Our day began in *Abuelita's* kitchen; it was our favorite room in her modest house. It was from the kitchen where the sounds of pots and pans clanged as she prepared for her morning chores. It was where she began to percolate a pot of coffee and began to make the tortillas for the day. She made the *tortillas en la frescura del día*, in the freshness of the day, she said often. The best time to make *tortillas* was before the Texas sun made the kitchen unbearably hot. *Para mi abuelita*, for my grandmother, it was the best time to do any work. Barefoot steps, mild thumps from the balls of my feet, delicate jumps, and pixie-hops were echoed by rattling knick-knacks in each room as I made my way into her kitchen. Hearing my approach, *Abuelita* anticipated my greeting.

"*Buenos días, Nana.*" I greeted her, "Good morning, Nana."

"*Buenos días, mi reina.*" She'd say good morning to me, calling me her queen.

Now, if you ask me, by all comparisons, there is no better way a grandmother can build self-esteem in her granddaughter. She was way ahead of her time with esteem building. She was wise that way.

Listening to the music from her kitchen radio, *Abuelita* swayed as she cooked. Our family loved to dance, most often at dance halls for weddings, anniversaries and benchmark birthday celebrations, like *quinceaneras*, which we called fifteen-year-old debuts, or "debuts," almost like a cotillion for a debutante. But our family also danced in *Abuelita's* house at reunions and Christmas. Occasionally, when my Uncle Henry heard radio music, he shuffled his way to *Abuelita*, grabbed her and danced a Mexican shuffle or two with her, more if she let him. Most often, she shuffled a few steps with him, before pushing him away at arm's length and returning to cooking. *Abuelita* danced in her kitchen, swaying as she stirred the food in the pan and listened to the radio.

The Zenith radio console's dial was set on a Spanish-speaking radio station. The famous voice of the radio announcer distinctly called out the station's call sign, KCOR. His comfortingly familiar voice reverberated in a diminishing echo, which I thought made him sound distinguished. Sometimes, I imitated the announcer and giggled with myself; other times, my cousins and I imitated his voice in unison, mimicking the echo we heard on the radio. A laugh was a good way to start any morning. When we got older, sometimes we still mimicked the announcer, always resulting in a memory-laced laugh. Early every morning KCOR played "Las Mañanitas," which literally translates as the little, sweet mornings. The traditional Mexican birthday song, it was sung over the generations, always very early in the day, just about the time the morning sun awakened the day. It was the best way to awaken a favorite relative or loved one to show them love on their birthday. Sometimes musicians were hired to play and sing "Las Mañanitas" at the birthday celebrant's bedroom window just as the last of the morning dew appeared on the grass. But most often in those days, "Las Mañanitas" dedications for birthday celebrants were made over the radio. It is a tradition that continues to this day. Then, as now, the song was played from a record produced by a Mariachi group. Sometimes, I stood by the radio just to listen to "Las Mañanitas." It will always be a feel-good song to me. Hearing it now, I remember the song coming from the old, floor-standing, wooden radio that was taller than I was then. The song reminded me that I would get older. Someday I'd grow up, outgrow the radio in height and become taller than my *Abulelita*.

Meanwhile, I went to wash my face and brush my teeth. While I waited for my grandmother to make breakfast, I ran through the kitchen and out the kitchen's back screen door into the backyard. A farm wire mesh fence ran along the perimeter of my grandmother's backyard. Strange as it seems, it was the fence dividing my grandmother's yard from my aunt Jesusita's yard. Yet, it was the same fence that connected the two families. We always knew who was the last person to talk over the fence, and here is how: when the fenced leaned toward my aunt's yard, then the last one to talk was from grandmother's side. When the fence leaned toward my grandmother's yard, the last one to talk was from my aunt's side. Most of the time, I leaned on the fence to make the first call of the day.

My call was for a morning meeting. "Laaaaaaaren, Miiiiiiiiia!" This was my morning call song to my two cousins closest to my age. Our meetings were held in the backyard between our homes where the wire mesh fence met a great big Texas mesquite tree, about halfway back from Ruiz Street. It was our favorite meeting place but also where grownups met for a brief chat. It all happened under the mesquite.

Lauren walked out the back screen door. The rusty spring on the screen door screeched until it stopped ricocheting off its frame and finally slammed shut. Just as it came to rest, Mia emerged through the same old door, causing the door spring to screech and the door to bounce again. We met at the fence in the morning shade beneath the large mesquite tree. There, my cousins and I made our plans for the day. It was where we planned who we would pretend to be for the day. Would we be teachers, mothers, nurses, or maybe even policewomen!? We already knew a policewoman.

Every school morning after our meeting, we cousins – all preschoolers – ran to a little slope at the end of a fence by the street. The three of us sat on the small slope and waited for the police lady. We saw her walking from several blocks down Ruiz Street. She came from direction of "*la tiendita de los chinitos,*" the Chinese grocery store where the owners called my grandmother "Mama." Sometimes the morning sun was so hot as we waited, perspiration drops rolled from our hairline down our temples onto our cheeks. We were patient and waited until she approached, walking toward us on the next block. When she reached the opposite side of our crosswalk, we began to giggle anxiously. We looked at each other, smiling and giggling. When the policewoman stood directly in front of us on the other side of the street, we stood up, waved to her and shouted. Yelling, hollering and calling out were all forms of daily communication in our *barrio.*

"Helloooo, policewoman, helloooo," we called out. She would respond with her right white-gloved hand, giving us a friendly wave. It was a gentle hand wave reserved just for young children. Oh, she was *so* important: defender and protector of young ones at school. One day, when we became old enough to go to school, she would be our protector and defender. It would make us proud that she was our protector.

She wore a navy blue skirt, a white crisply starched blouse buttoned all the way to her neck. A white cloth sash crossed from her left shoulder down to the right side of her waist, where it was attached to a waistband of the same width and material. Right over her heart she wore a bright shiny silver badge of honor, *una insignia de honor.* Sometimes, when the sun shone brightly at just the right angle on her badge, we three stood up to salute her. Solemnly, she raised her right white gloved hand to her headgear and returned the salute. We put our hands down and giggled with the thrill of it all. She smiled as she continued her walk to the end of the block where she resumed helping young children cross the street to the Eli Men Terry School. Deflated, we retreated to breakfast at Grandmother's before immersing ourselves in the pretend world of the day.

We lived in the city *barrios*. Each family had a chicken coop in the backyard. *Mi tia Jesusita y tio Humberto*, my aunt and uncle, had a large chicken coop to supply eggs for their large family. *Abuelita* had a smaller coop to support herself and a visiting grandchild now and then.

One particular summer, *Tio Humberto* built an additional coop. The new coop was guest quarters of the exotic nomadic fowls they called geese, *se llamaban gansos*. The new coop became home to an especially noisy specimen of this exotic variety. I know because during our morning chats, Lauren or Mia, one of them, remembered the *gansos* in the coop. It was Mia who – very gingerly – checked to see if their goose had laid an egg. Lauren wouldn't dare look under that fractious bird!

Easily frightened, Lauren was the family scaredy cat. When Lauren was bitten by an insect, she'd run screaming all over the backyard, around the fruit trees. We never knew which fruit tree she would run around first and maybe she didn't either. Sometimes she began running around the pear tree, then onto the peach tree, around the pecan tree onto the plum tree or the fig tree. At times, she ran around the chosen tree several times. Other times, we just never knew; but eventually she ran back around the patio furniture and around the clothesline waving her hands in the air just because an insect had bitten her. So if a goose would have pecked her, she probably would have done the same thing. Now, of course, Lauren is older, matured, sophisticated ... and she still is easily excited when an insect bites her.

So it was Mia who checked to see if the goose had laid an egg. Oh, we were not looking for a golden egg. We had not heard that story yet. Any egg would do. Mia repeated her daring search every morning.

After one of our morning meetings, I went inside to eat breakfast, and sat at the table with a sad face.

Abuelita asked, "*¿Y por qué está tan triste, mi reina,*" why is my queen so sad?

"*Es porque Lauren y Mía tienen un ganso y yo no tengo ni una.*" The only explanation that could be given was "... Lauren and Mia have a goose and I have none."

"*Ah, se paciente.*" She only gave me her words of wisdom, to "Be patient; all in its time."

"*Sí, Abuelita.*" I said quietly and waited for my breakfast.

It took a day to build a coop in my grandmother's backyard. The next day there was a goose in the cage. Some people may say it was a matter of keeping up with the Joneses; but in our neighborhood there was very little "keeping up" and no Joneses at all. There, one might have been accused of "keeping up with the Martinez family."

At the next morning's meeting Mia went to check for a goose egg. It was true there was a goose egg to show Lauren and me. Suddenly, I remembered that *I too had a goose.* I skipped across the backyard to check the cage. There was the goose ... but no egg! I walked sadly to meet my cousins by the mesquite tree. The sun made perspiration beads on my face and nose. There was nothing to report.

The following morning there was nothing for me to report. So it went for a couple of days. When I slouched waiting for my breakfast, my grandmother asked why I was so sad.

"*Y hoy, ¿por qué estás tan triste?*" She asked.

"*El ganso de Lauren y Mia pone huevos y mi ganso está rota, no pone huevos.*" I explained that Lauren and Mia's goose laid eggs, and my goose was broken. It didn't make eggs.

"*Ah se paciente y tenga fe. Todo en su tiempo.*" Once again, she shared her wisdom. She told me to "Be patient: have faith, and everything in its time."

One nice morning again after our routine meeting, I walked to my goose's cage. The goose was there all right, just sitting ... doing nothing! I jerked around to scamper and report to my cousins. As I turned, my eyes widened in amazement, the goose moved ... and there it was! A goose egg! I opened the cage door, shooed the goose away and gathered the precious egg. With one hand, I cradled the precious egg. With the other, I closed the cage door.

Turning toward my cousins, who waited by the fence, I could hardly speak. "It's an egg!" I squealed. "*Es un huevo!*" I was thrilled and excited to see the egg! My arm was extended in front of me; my hand was cradling the delicate egg. Quickly, proudly, I marched all the way across the backyard to meet my cousins by the tree. They were as amazed as I was.

Next, we compared goose eggs. Their egg was a little bigger than mine. But, it didn't matter, my goose was perfect. We were all happy about our morning production. It was time for breakfast and time to show my grandmother what our goose had produced.

I went in to the kitchen squealing and told her to look at the egg that I now cradled in both hands.

"*Mire, mire nana, es un huevo!*" She heard me say "look, look Nana, it is an egg!"

"*Ya veo* ..." She smiled, showed how pleased she was. She repeated joyously, "...*ya veo.*" She had seen my goose's egg.

That was quite a summer. My cousins and I recall it as the summer of the miracle, *del milagro*.

The visiting geese, even though they produced eggs, didn't stay around long at the Martinez house. Perhaps they were just too exotic to remain on Ruiz Street. Just like the chickens, they just didn't stay long in the cages. I was told my fowl was given away after the miracle.

Later, my cousin Rudy said to me.

"Your goose didn't lay an egg."

"Oh yes, it did!" I said.

"Oh no, it didn't!" He argued.

"Oh yes, iiiiit did!" I said as I stomped my foot on the ground.

"Oh no, it didn't! Ganders can't lay eggs!" He smartly snapped back.

I happen to know my goose did lay an egg because sometimes miracles do happen.

It was known that mi *abuelita podía hacer milagros con sus manos*, my grandmother could perform miracles with her hands. I was very lucky because as the folk healer, faith healer in our *barrio*, she helped me realize the thrill and delight of owning a goose for the first time. And the faith I badly needed in those days and in many more days to come. I realized it that summer when it happened with the miracle of Ruiz Street – *el milagro de la calle Ruiz.*

IV

The Hunt for the Golden Yellow King Edward Box

Excitement!

There was excitement! Before we could even speak English, before we even knew what excitement meant, before we knew it took letters to spell the exciting word in any language! It was there, *en el barrio*, in our Westside neighborhood in San Antonio, Texas. It was there – excitement!

In a late 1950s summer when the Texas heat could still be tolerated, my cousins and I knew we were on the threshold to a new world. The ceremonial introduction to our passage of life was our hunt – a hunt for an empty golden yellow King Edward box. My hunt began at *"la tiendita,"* our neighborhood corner convenience store (which we also called Mrs. Morgan's). The front of her frame house had been converted into a small store. She lived in the back of the house with her grandson. Mrs. Morgan was of German heritage but spoke only English. My heritage was Mexican-Native American and I only spoke Spanish. So when I shopped in Mrs. Morgan's store, we usually used primitive communication. We used sign language, our very own special sign language, which was made up of pointing, nodding yes or no and smiling. Sometimes we just shared friendly frustrated glances about our awkward miscommunication.

I suppose Mrs. Morgan's convenience store's daily inventory was like most neighborhood mom-and-pop stores in that time. I seldom noticed what bread, milk or eggs mothers and grannies placed in their shopping bags, much less what men might slip into a pocket after paying. When I went in her store, I had eyes only for a big glass jar capped with a worn red metal lid that sat high on a counter, beyond the reach of preschoolers. The clear glass jar was where she stored molasses cookies with white icing. Sometimes my hoarded pennies and nickels were enough to allow me to pick out my own cookie straight from the glass jar next to Mrs. Morgan's shiny cash register. The rest of the time, I looked to see if she had a small paper cylinder carton of salted peanuts that contained a coin as a prize. *Es cierto!* It is really true; coins like a shiny penny, nickel or dime! On rare occasion, the prize might even be a George Washington quarter when we got lucky. For peanuts, it was like a kid's lottery. And most often, it was my best buy.

Mrs. Morgan's store opened early in the morning. Soon after, I arrived and placed my latest peanut winnings on the scratched glass counter. It was a salty nickel! Stepping back, she gave me a glance over her Benjamin Franklin glasses. Then she glanced at the coin on the glass counter. If the coin was salty, Mrs. Morgan knew I was buying something for myself. She knew it was not errand money. By wiggling my pointing finger to and fro, I directed her attention to the next glass case over.

Tapping on the glass with one knuckle, I used the pointing finger of my other hand to indicate the King Edward Cigar box inside the glass case. She reached in and tapped the edge of the hard pressed cardboard box. I smiled and nodded my head up and down. Yes! Beneath her white-haired eyebrows, one of her clear blue eyes winked in confirmation. That little wink always followed her comprehension of what I wanted to buy. She smiled broadly ... then Mrs. Morgan pulled out – a cigar!

My head shook urgently from side to side. *No comprende!* She had misunderstood; I could not believe it! But then I heard her muffled laughter, which made me feel a little better; there was no misunderstanding. I was surprised by her rare playfulness. Every now and then when she felt she had been surprised by a quiet customer, Mrs. Morgan rushed into the store from the rooms at the back where she lived. Once, she walked into her store with a frankfurter hanging from her mouth like a cigar! Even though she was the first business woman I got to know, Mrs. Morgan was not all business.

We smiled at each other over the glass counter because we had reached a quiet understanding. She winked again as she emptied the few cigars remaining in the box and replaced them in a row inside the counter. Mrs. Morgan's beautiful eyes sparkled when she glanced again at the eager little girl before her. She carried the brightly printed box back to the cash register. I often thought that her stool behind the cash register was her favorite place in the store, because it was where she took care of business. But she surprised me again. She put the salty nickel in the cigar box, then closed it. Next, she leaned forward and carefully placed the King Edward cigar box in my summer tanned preschool hands. What a real surprise! In my inestimable delight, I presented Mrs. Morgan with an ear-to-ear toothless grin.

"*Gracias.*" I thanked her.

The white-haired businesswoman saw me wrap my skinny arms around the multi-colored box. Hugging the box tightly before she changed her mind, I walked out of her place of business a happy customer. The store bell chimed above the screen door as I left. In my dreamy thoughts, the screen door bell was proudly chiming, rejoicing for my successful hunt! I stepped out onto the top step. With the cigar box held in a vise-grip close to my chest in one hand, I grasped the screen door handle with the other and closed the worn screen door quietly. A faded rainbow of a Rainbow Bread advertisement adorned Mrs. Morgan's dusty screen door. That day, a different "pot of gold" went beyond the screen door rainbow on the door, in the form of a golden yellow King Edward cigar box for one *mestizo* kid.

I hesitated on the top step thinking ... wondering about my cousins and *their* hunt for *their* King Edward cigar boxes. Maybe they would find their boxes at "*la tiendita de los chinitos,*" the Chinese grocery store a couple of blocks up the street. Maybe they would find theirs at the Mexican family grocery store several blocks the other way. There was diversity in our *barrio*; it was with the store owners. Our local shopkeepers were happy to help us anytime. But, this late summer was different. All the store owners knew of our excitement for the passages that were about to consume our young lives. They knew that several of us, cousins and other *niños del barrio*, children in the neighborhood, were about to begin our first year of public school. To each of us, it was a new passage of life. All of us were preparing to leave our *barrio* kitchens on the day of the hunt. And our passages could only properly begin with the hunt for empty King Edward cigar boxes.

I took another step down and began to walk home with the cigar box close to my heart. We, cousins, would meet later for sure. When we did, we would compare our hunting adventures. But for now, Mrs. Morgan and I had taken care of business. She had a happy customer who would long remember her kindness. In her heart, as well as in her businesswoman's head, Mrs. Morgan knew the value of good customer service. It was just good business and still is. Even though she is long gone, her business acumen and ethics often return to my mind.

My hunt was over, but it did not pacify the excitement that was still there in my *barrio*.

V

Los Colores, The Colors

En casa, at home, the golden yellow box from my hunt held a place of honor on a living room table where it sat, waiting. That prized box would play a central role in a day that was soon to come. Proud parents gave my cousins and I each a big Red Chief tablet with paper lined in blue ink, where we knew that we would learn to make our letters. Grandmothers, grandfathers, aunts or uncles added a jar of white paste glue and one school bus yellow pencil, its fresh pink eraser tip untarnished. Lucky ones among us received a lacquered wooden ruler, which was a measurement of status, or so we thought.

Then, before we burst with excitement, we were each given a three-by-four-inch green and yellow box. Inside its colorful exterior, the box contained eight new brilliantly colored waxed sticks uniquely wrapped with tinted paper. They were called Crayola crayons. Crayola sounded Spanish. *Brincamos, para arriba y para abajo.* Oh yes! We jumped up and down squealing, thrilled with owning our very own Crayolas, as if the colors defined our status, our worthiness and our success. Later, we learned Crayolas were also called crayons. We simply called them "colors," *colores*.

My Crayola box went into the golden yellow King Edward cigar box along with the school bus yellow pencil. The rest of the school supplies went into my red and black tartan plaid book satchel. I beamed, knowing that my appearance had now taken on a sophisticated new aspect because *now I was old enough to go to school.*

We discovered the crayons had their own first names, too. Brown, black, red, yellow, green, blue, orange and violet (but we called it purple). Their last name was Crayon. *¿Cuál sería el más favorito?* "Which would become our favorite one?" There were so many Crayolas. Wow, eight colors! We celebrated the excitement. We celebrated fulfilling the long yearning of having a box of "colors" to call our very own. Those of us beginning our new world, *creíamos que éramos mucho*, we were proud. We thought we were *big stuff* because we had our very own freshly dressed crayons. Today, some might say we thought "we were all that." Oh yes! We were so modestly proud without shame.

There would be no more pretending to be coloring. Our coloring would become defined with time.

No more coloring with generations of broken-necked and half-necked crayon bits from *Abuelita's* stash. Her treasure, *Abuelita's* stash of worn crayon stubs, was now passed to us. It had become our watch.

Oh yes! We would miss her treasured stash kept in a small crinkled brown paper bag. We would miss the scents of the old colorful stubs. Those scents were a link with the delicate memories of those relatives who colored with them, touched them before we did. *Abuelita* had collected and treasured them, tokens once touched by our aunts, uncles and a few older cousins who had already made the journey before us.

Now there were eight brilliant colors for our untainted minds to choose for our lives' untinted canvases. Yet, it was up to us to give the Crayolas their worthiness, brilliance and success. On our journeys, we would make our own colorful lives. We'd add our own stubs to *Abuelita's* stash of colors in the same crinkled paper bag. All that came later.

We, with our majestic Crayolas, were beginning a journey into a new world with a new language we had yet to learn. The language would change our lives into what would be a lifetime of learning. It was our parents and grandparents who taught us language, before the world of teachers, phonics, see and say and other vehicles for learning the mechanics of language. In our neighborhood, it was a simple language.

My generation of cousins and I were non-English speakers. But just before the first day of school, *Abuelita* gave me a very watered down basic English class to prepare me for my very first day of school. This was Project Head Start, when there was none! A crash course was given the night before the first day of school, an orientation for the following morning. That was it! That was all there was. She said phrases and I was to repeat them. Once.

Here was my *Abuelita's* course in English, with translation:

"*Si quieres algo, dices,* 'please.'" = If you want something, you say "please."

"*Si las maestras te dan algo, dices,* 'tank yous.'" = If the teachers give you something, you say "thank you."

"*Si te dicen algo, dices 'jes m'am o no m'am.'*" = If they say something to you, you say, "yes m'am or no m'am."

Abuelita, with her very limited English, prepared me with the language of social skills, eight little vocabulary words to take with me into the new world along with the eight wonderful bright colors.

On the first day of our new adventure, we cousins met at my *Abuelita's* house. The school was two houses from my grandmother's house down and across Ruiz Street. Ruiz was perpendicular to the campus and we had to cross two streets. *Abuelita* told me, as the oldest, to hold my cousins' hands. She looked me in the eye and said they were my responsibility. After instructing us to walk on the sidewalk (where there was a sidewalk), she gave us her blessing, making the sign of the cross as she intoned, "*En el nombre del Padre, el Hijo y el Espíritu Santo, Amen.*"

We all walked with our hands joined, smiling, yet not really knowing how to act now that we were finally going to Eli Men Terry School. It was so strange leaving *Abuelita's* house without her holding my hand. Suddenly, an unexpected curious thought crossed my mind. I stopped very abruptly at the edge of *Abuelita's* yard with my cousins. An urgent concern had invaded my mind. I turned around and ran back with cousins in tow, returning to my *abuelita*.

She stood on the high porch watching over us. With innocent, searching eyes, I looked up at her and asked, "*¿Abuelita, y cómo sabremos cuando venir a la casa?*" Suddenly it was a rather urgent thought that I know when it was time to come home from school. Surely we had to get back home. I was responsible; when could I lead my cousins back home? She told me the bell would ring and when it did, it would be the time to come back home. So now I knew what to do to get back home and it was important for me to know such things. She gave more instructions. *Abuelita* told me to wait for my cousins after school by the school gate, then to hold hands again and wait for the lady. She meant for us to wait for the policewoman to help us cross the street after school. *Abuelita* blessed us once more. Satisfied that we could not get too many blessings from *Abuelita*, we turned and were on our way to school – again!

We walked past the two houses to the end of our block. Finally the day had come. We knew the day would come; we just had to wait our turn. The policewoman found herself serving, protecting and defending her little fan club. As the policewoman crossed the street to come for us, we smiled in unison and greeted her. We admired her neat uniform and her friendly smile. I had a lot of respect and admiration for the police lady and was proud to know her, in spite of the fact that I never learned her name. We were so familiar, it somehow seemed unnecessary. She led us across Ruiz Street, then across the other street, bringing us safely to the Eli Men Terry School. She smiled all the while as she led us across each street. Having her looking over us was like having our own protective angel in a blue uniform. Once we were safely at the school gate, we turned, smiled and waved goodbye to her. She returned our waves and smiles. Then she saluted us. We were surprised by her gesture. We turned, our hands linked in solidarity. We entered the grounds, then the building for and of our education.

Our solidarity was short-lived. In a school campus two blocks long, we cousins were separated by the distance between our assigned classrooms. In my room, the Anglo teacher talked all day long. To whatever the teachers said to me, my response was "jes m'am o no m'am," followed by a toothless grin. It made me happy to use the English that Abuelita had taught me the night before. My teacher often looked confused; I didn't understand why. I was speaking *Abuelita's* English. It was a little annoying not being understood.

What seemed like a lifetime of learning was called "the first day of school!" I thought we had learned everything we needed to learn, all on the first day of school. The bell rang and it was time to go home. The teacher took us all outside in a straight line. When she released us, I knew she let us go because all the children scattered. So did I, in my all new, monkey-see, monkey-do world. I saw my cousin Lauren coming out of school with her class. Then they scattered and so did she. We saw each other and ran to meet. I took Lauren's hand and then I found my cousin Gregorio. I took his hand, too. We walked to the school gate. Oh my, the policewoman was not there! Now it was up to me to get us across the streets. It was a little scary though I trusted myself to get us across the two streets safely. I was a big girl and knew it because I was a proud owner of a King Edward pencil box, colors and a book satchel. I looked both ways; there were no cars forever. We ran across once. Then we crossed again. We continued to walk safely on the sidewalk and onto *Abuelita's* house. My cousins went on to their houses down the street. I watched them go as I walked on the front sidewalk to *Abuelita's* house.

My grandmother often kept the front screen door unlocked. She only locked it when we took our afternoon nap, our *siesta de la tarde.* I walked into my grandmother's house quietly and found her in the kitchen, where she was standing over the sink washing breakfast dishes, humming a song to them. She was startled when she heard my voice.

"*Ya he legado.*" In a matter of fact tone, she learned that "I had arrived."

She turned around immediately with her mouth wide open. I never saw her look that way before. For sure my words had contributed to the expression she had on her face. She asserted that school was not over. I said that the bell had rung, which was when school was over – according to her own explanation. To my consternation, *Abuelita* ordered me to go back to school. Drying her plump hands on a bleached muslin apron, she took my first grade hand and led me out the front screen door in a hurry. As we walked uncomfortably fast, she clarified that the first school bell was the *recess bell* not the "school is out" bell. Well now, this just really confused me. How was I going to tell the school bells apart? For goodness sake, I was almost a dropout on the first day of school!

When we got to the front porch, my other cousins had made their way back to *Abuelita's* house. My *Tia Jesusita* called out from her house to my *Abuelita,* as was common in *el barrio.* *Tia* let my grandmother know we had to go back to school. It was only the recess bell. So once again, we met at the end of the sidewalk, linked up our hands and made our way back to school safely without the policewoman.

Three teachers saw us making our second crossing to school. Looking frightened, they hurried to meet us. Oh, yes, running in the opposite direction did cross my mind! But I was responsible for my cousins and I knew that responsibility came with consequences. One teacher scolded us, which mattered very little because we didn't understand her anyway. We could, however, tell that she was displeased. The other unhappy teacher spoke slowly, gently trying to explain something to us. It also didn't matter because we didn't understand her English either, even without the scolding. I already knew that I had made a mistake as the leader of the pack. The mistake had already been explained to me in Spanish by *mi abuelita*. Thereafter, the teachers kept a close watch on us during lunch recess, afternoon recess and for several days afterward during recess regardless of the time of day. We were teaching them as they were teaching us.

Our education began with learning the difference between the various school bells. We had yet more learning to do. I guessed that this was the first step, the introduction into a lifetime of learning the ways of this new world called school.

As the first school year progressed, my cousins and I learned a little more English. Although we spoke Spanish in school and during recess, the teachers made it pretty clear to us we must "speak English." This became ever clearer to me.

One day, Lauren and I saw our older cousin, Esperanza, swinging on the monkey bars with some of her friends under a mesquite tree in the middle of the school yard. Esperanza has always been very pretty. Her pretty smile has always been a welcomed sight. She was five years older than we were. We were in awe of her years of experience and her beauty, knowing that she would always be a lovely and much-loved elder. Lauren and I decided to go talk to Esperanza. We linked hands and ran across the playground shouting her name. Lauren and I giggled and greeted Esperanza in Spanish. She smiled and in a congenial manner explained to us that we were not supposed to speak Spanish in school.

She put everything in perspective and said, "English, we must speak English. No Spanish in school. *No hablamos español en la escuela.* Ok?" She was already bilingual! I supposed she spoke Spanish slowly and softly to make certain there were no misunderstandings.

We were not supposed to be in that part of the school yard either, she also explained that to us in a pleasant way. We gave her a hug, an integral family custom with us when parting from relatives. As if on cue, all three of us said our goodbyes in English, in unison. Lauren and I linked hands as we ran back to our section of the school yard. When we got to our designated play area, we looked back at Esperanza. She was smiling and waving to us. Our hands were still linked. We smiled and waved back to her with our free hands. I learned about boundaries at school that day. Even more lessons about boundaries would present themselves throughout our school years.

I guessed we were not allowed to speak Spanish in school because once during my first year of school it caused a lot of confusion. My cousins and I called each other *"hermanita"* and "*hermanito.*" The Anglo teachers soon discovered we were calling each other "little brother" and "little sister." Soon, there was a "little" investigation at the Eli Men Terry School to resolve why there were so many of us brothers and sisters all in the same grade, with different shades of brown-colored features and different last names. Mystery solved! We, cousins, were all summoned to the front office. We didn't have to know enough English to know this was *not* a good thing. When the talking box they called an intercom declared "... to the principal's office," the students' gasps made me aware it *really* was not a good thing. I arrived at the office first. The teachers' faces often spoke silent words during my first year of school. Faces were doing just that when I arrived at the front office. Soon Lauren walked into the office, stepping softly. Gosh! *that* was a good idea; I should have done that, too. Maybe I would leave softly. I was already planning my departure without knowing why we were in the principal's office. Lauren and I quickly joined hands. It had become our solidarity gesture, a memorably part of our first school year. In the principal's office, we were told to call each other by our "God-given" names. I was a little confused and asked.

"Is not our 'God-given' names brothers and sisters?"

I was already learning English, and I was a little bold with it. The moment the expression on our teachers' faces shifted, my comfort shifted also. One of the teachers' eyebrows seemed to transform from two black minus signs into a black letter V, and her eyes were not happy eyes either. My expressed thoughts had married what I was learning in English at school and the Catechism I was learning at church. Perhaps I would have been better off spouting off *Abuelita's* English. I desperately wished I had said "Please, jes m'am o no m'am, tank yous" and smiled. The office room surely could have used more smiling faces and fewer V-shaped eyebrows about that time. They could have easily been the prototype for the Angry Birds characters. We were sent back to our classrooms. Lauren started to sob. She cried when she was frightened. It seemed important that one of us should stifle her tears and try to understand what the Anglo teachers were telling us.

As the responsible cousin, I said, "*No llores Lauren, no llores. Es okay.*" While I was not sure speaking to Lauren in Spanish was a good idea, I knew it was more crucial that Lauren understand what I was saying. I pleaded with her to stop crying. It saddened me to let go of her hand when, alone, she returned to her room. Gigantic tears rolled down from her big hazel eyes. A wrinkled brow of worry framed her eyes as, tearfully, she shot a look my way. Full of worry about her, I tried to avoid crying, too. One of us must not cry; I remember thinking that. *One of us must not cry.*

A relief from misunderstandings about English and school bells came when teacher announced singing or coloring time. We learned to sing *My Country 'Tis of Thee (America).* We pledged allegiance to the United States of America as we put our *mestizo* hands over our assimilating hearts. We did this every morning. Some of the school customs were incomprehensible mysteries to me. I just repeated the actions and the words, as were the customs. That was how I learned at school. It was "a monkey-see, monkey-do world" for some of us from *el barrio.*

One autumn day, our teacher gave the class a basic bold outlined picture of the United States flag waving for coloring practice. The flag was red, white and blue, I knew it. Respect and pride for the American flag was taught to me at home before I even started school. I understood how proud we should be of the United States of America flag. I had already heard stories about my uncle, Staff Sergeant Vicente Montez Barron, who died in World War II. A handsome picture of him hung in a place of honor on *Abuelita's* living room wall. My grandmother, like so many next-of-kin of that era, had received the United States flag because my *Tio Vicente* had made the ultimate sacrifice in serving his country. I knew the flag was to be honored and colored red, white and blue.

On another day, my teacher gave the class a different bold outlined picture of a man she called Benjamin Franklin. It was more coloring practice for us. It did not take much of my time or much of my brown Crayola to color his hair. But it took almost all of my brown Crayola to finish making *el Señor* Franklin look Mexican!

We had begun our journey with young fresh minds, agile young bodies, some of us with a mouthful of teeth and some with toothless grins. It was a simple time. We were innocent and inexperienced just like a new box of freshly dressed crayons. We had begun with a colorful excitement toward our adventures and transitions. A new language, many kinds of new learning, the panoply of life presented itself in many hues, just like a box of Crayola crayons.

VI

Just Like Any Kid

Just like any kid during the late 1950s, I was at the age of innocent reasoning and in the midst of harvesting teeth. I was made in Mexico, born in America, the land of liberty. Just like any kid of that time who only spoke Spanish, I went to school and learned to read, write and speak English.

Yes, they called me Mexican in school and later they called me bilingual. I guessed it was because I must have been pretty good at speaking Dutch or something. My teacher told me to be a Dutch girl in our autumn PTA presentation. Dutch and English sounded the same to me and I guessed that they were. "*Pero eres Mexicana,*" my grandmother reminded me I was Mexican by family heritage.

After memorizing my part, I had to prepare myself for the presentation. I began by bathing at my grandmother's house. She had a big white oval tub with legs that looked like a lion's paws. We brushed our teeth over the tub. Our own rinse glasses were next to an empty Folgers coffee can. We dipped the old tin can in a galvanized tin bucket filled with water. We called it the dipping can and used it to rinse ourselves. Though once *someone* got a fancy notion and it was only one time. That *someone* took an ice pick and made holes on the bottom of the dipping can. When the dipping can was dipped and filled with water, it became a shower. My *Abuelita* made it clear that she was not pleased. While she was taking a bath, I heard her shriek from the bathroom.

The eroded Palmolive soap bar was next to the dipping can. And there by the Palmolive soap were our *estropajos*. An *estropajo* is a rustic version of a modern-day bathing loofah or scourer. My *mestiza* grandmother, *mi abuelita*, made our rough *estropajos* by using flaxen-colored shipping twine and pulling the sisal twine threads apart until it resembled a small bird nest. We bathed with her homemade rough scouring pads, her *estropajos*, instead of soft washcloths.

There were assorted tub cleanser cans lined up on the tub's rim, leaning against the wall. Why *Abuelita* kept an assortment of cleansers is still a mystery to me. Perhaps they had individual uses ... or perhaps they resulted from advertised specials my grandmother could not resist. In any case, my grandmother kept them lined up next to our *estropajos*. I studied the image of a Dutch girl on the Dutch Girl scouring cleanser can. She wore a big white Dutch girl's hat, which I compared in my imagination with the white veil I wore to Sunday Mass. My hair was not yellow like hers, but brown with multicolored ribbons woven into my braids, *con listónes tejidos en mis trenzas*. *It was* a Mexican girl tradition. On the can, the Dutch girl wore a pretty blue dress with a white apron. I wore multicolored dresses that my grandmother made for me. Sometimes I wore

Abuelita's worn white apron wrapped around me twice, much like her arms that wrapped around me.

The Dutch girl's skin color was almost the color of my mother's Mexican skin, the color of fading gardenias. On the other hand, my skin color changed with the seasons. In the summer, I had cinnamon-colored skin, or as we say, *piel como el color de canela*. In another comparison, the Dutch Girl wore big wooden shoes, while I wore shiny black shoes that squeaked and sometimes ate my ruffled socks.

Now that I could read (!!), I grabbed a cleanser can and read, "chases dirt." I wondered if maybe this was the same cleanser whose song bragged, "It cleans as it whitens." By tilting the cleanser can, it was easy to dust little dots of white power on my *estropajo*. I did so and the scrubbing began, chasing dirt away, off my body. Secretly, I thought my dark skin color would also fade.

Mi *abuelita* walked in the bathroom and immediately exclaimed, "*Balgame! ¿Y qué estás haciendo?*" This hardly needs a translation because we, as children, have all heard this universal question from our elders or teachers regardless of our heritage. I have had my share of this question in my lifetime. My *abuelita* exclaimed, "And what are you doing?" She was a little shocked. I never learned the literal translation for *Balgame*, but I suppose it has the same connotation as "By golly!"

"*¿Sabe qué? Esto no trabaja.¡No tiene valor! ¡Ningún valor!*" The spoken words of frustration come out of my mouth. I had made my testimonial. The cleanser "did not work, it was worthless!" This definitely was not the cleanser that sang "it cleans as it whitens" – I was still the color of cinnamon!

Just before the PTA program, the teacher reminded me to remove my ribbons from my hair. Swaying her long index finger from side to side, her high-pitched, theatrically sweet voice sang, "Consuelo, no ribbons."

I attended the PTA presentation with my bleach-scented reasoning, burgundy-highlighted skin and *no ribbons in my braids.* As I portrayed a Dutch girl wearing a big white Dutch hat, I was more aware than ever that I was a *mestiza* (Mexican) faced girl with distinctly non-blonde braids. The wooden shoes on my feet were not my comfortable Mexican sandals, *huaraches,* either. They belonged to a culture other than the Anglo majority, but I was aware that it was not *my* culture.

Just like any kid of the late 1950s, I traveled with my family to visit relatives in the summer. The journey from Texas to Alabama was an endurance test for a child who could not see over the back of the front seat where my parents enjoyed vistas unknown to me. So I laid down on the back seat with my head resting on the palms of my hands and my legs crossed at the ankles. Bored, I made up an activity to occupy the time. Mine was not a car game; it was a car chant. Mother sometimes called it a "broken record." With eyes wandering to occasional traffic lights, gas station signs and a seemingly unending procession of tree tops (all I could see out the car windows from my reclining position), I watched thousands of evergreen trees race by against the blue Mississippi sky. About once every eleven minutes, I squeaked plaintively, "are we there yet?" Mesmerized with the highlights and shadows of trees flashing, I chanted,

"Dark, light, light, light,
dark, light, railroad, light,
light, dark, dark, dark, dark"

until I finally fell asleep.

Eventually, the warmth of the sun touched my eyes and awakened me. The sense of being alone in the car urged me to sit up. I *was* alone. There was nothing for me to do but cross my arms and lean on the back of the long front plastic car seat. Outside, sun rays peeked out from behind a cloud. I watched as the sun rays touched a little piece of paper on the car's dash board. Curiosity caused my cinnamon-stick legs to fly over the back of the long front seat, thrusting me into a sitting position. With both hands, I grabbed the note. I could read!

Mom's printed, simple words, the note read:

Come inside.
Love,
Mom

Tossing the note aside, I grabbed a shiny chrome lever on the door with both hands and pushed the car door open. As my feet jumped onto the metal running board, I thought, *Inglés*! English! That metal running board ran nowhere!

After jumping off the metal running board, so typical of cars in those days, I took the shiny, chrome handle on the outside of the car door with both of my hands, and anchored my feet in gravel. Pushing with my slingshot arm muscles and skinny leg muscles (and with my body angled at forty-five degrees), I pushed the car door shut.

My brown eyes did their Felix-the-Cat-clock search. Those big brown eyes turned, leading my head then my body to see what was behind me. There stood a gray weathered building with a long, uneven porch on the front. Wooden steps, also uneven, led to the wooden porch. My feet ran up the steps and across the porch, where I grabbed a thin screen door handle and opened the door.

Inside, there was an Anglo couple dining at a table.

Behind a long dining counter stood a frowning man. His white clothes and large white apron (which I noticed wrapped around him only once) told me he was the restaurant man. Still frowning, he lifted a freakishly small white hat for a moment to mop his forehead. Compared to the Dutch girl's hat I had worn in the PTA presentation, his hat seemed small – like Popeye's hat in the cartoon. I told myself that if he wore a Dutch girl's hat, then he would look really silly! His hat was like the ice cream man's hat, the ice cream man whose old, white truck snaked slowly through our neighborhood, *en el barrio*, on summer days.

A man swiveled on a dining counter stool to see who had walked in. He stared blankly at the little dark-skinned girl who stood in the doorway looking for her parents. Scanning the room from left to right, I found my folks sitting at a booth near the back. Stepping forward toward them, I realized the rustic floorboards were mocking my squeaky shoes, those same shoes that sometimes ate my socks. No matter how slowly and quietly I tried to step, my shoes were joined by the loose floorboards in a mocking chorus. Step by embarrassingly squeaky step, I made my way to my folks. It reminded me of the time I had walked across my *abuelita's* freshly waxed kitchen floor, under her disapproving gaze. A sweating glass of ice water stood before each of my parents, and beside the water, each had already been served a cup of creamed coffee on a saucer.

Mi mama me preguntó. When my mother asked, I answered, "I want pancakes and milk. Pancakes and milk; that's what I want."

Suddenly the front screen door slammed shut. The man all dressed in white came from behind the counter, drying his hands on the white apron that wrapped around him only once. He came to our table and profoundly placed his hands on the table as if the table needed to be held down. He was scary. He looked at my Anglo stepdad and spoke firmly.

"You can stay."

Then, the man looked at me with his big, big dark eyes with bushy eyebrows. I hid my toothless grin with my small brown hands crisscrossed over my mouth. He looked at my dad again and spoke to my dad.

"She has to leave!"

I did not understand. Silently, I thought to myself: why do I have to leave? I had other teeth to eat with! I did not understand. I ... did ... not ... understand.

My dad had an answer for the man. He said, "If she goes, we all go."

The man with the white hat repeated his demand, still holding the table down.

Then the man in white stepped back from the table to make room for us to leave. My mother, my father and I each stood up slowly. Each of my folks took one of my small *mestizo* hands into theirs. I turned around to look at the man one last time. He stood, feet apart so that I saw a triangle between his legs. The muscles in his arms stood still and his hands sat on his waist. We left quietly.

Back in the car, I was excited about seeing my new aunts, uncles, grandparents and cousins. It was our first trip to visit my Anglo stepfather's people. What would my new grandmother be like? As I listened to muffled conversation from the front seat, which I knew was tense because of what had just happened in the diner, I still believed that *Diosito*, the creator, made people just like my mother's cookies: some light, others slightly brown and still others are a little overcooked, just like my Uncle Chocolate in San Antonio, Texas.

It was America in the 1950s; we were on a mysterious road journey – and another journey at the same time. A much more complicated journey.

Just like any kid of the late 1950s, I asked again, "Are we there yet?"

VII

Quite a Ways From Texas

We were no longer *Abuelita* and I; mother had remarried. Now, we were my mother, my stepdad and me. Eventually, we moved away from San Antonio to Killeen, Texas, a small town in central Texas where we were determined to begin anew as a family.

Maybe I should have exclaimed like my grandmother, "*Balgame! ¿Y de donde vienes?!*" But I didn't, I simply asked my new dad, "Where do you come from, where does your family live?" It was not like the thought of a "new daddy store" had escaped my quirky imagination.

The thought vanished when he answered, "Quite a ways from Texas." I was soon to learn many things about my stepdad and my new *familia*.

I called him "Dad." His family lived in a place he called "the backward part of the country." Sometimes he called it Huntsville, Alabama. Halfway through the twentieth century very few *mestizo*-faced people, like me, knew of Alabama. I didn't even know what "the backward part of the country" really meant.

My life experiences of seven years were not as limited as my English. To me, English words were strange and meaningless sounds when used in a phrase or sentence. But English was not the only language with confusing or meaningless words. Sometimes Spanish words were meaningless to me, too. That's when I would get into trouble. I found the Anglo ways and language difficult.

Sometimes, the language was easy to understand, like when my parents said, "Let's go."

When my mother remarried, she did not choose a Mexican-American. She picked a man from an Anglo family, and from an Anglo family in a different state, at that! It was clear from the outset that we would make a long drive to meet this new, light-skinned family. What could make this adventure extra special? A new car! In our driveway sat a brand new 1955 white and black Ford Fairlane that clearly inspired pride in my mother and my new stepfather. My dad said it had a nice chrome grill front and whitewall tires. He said it was nice, but not too colorful, and that's just what they instructed me to say about it, if asked. I memorized its colors out loud, "white and black," until my mom corrected me, saying, "Cars are painted not colored."

Dad said that faraway in Detroit, our new Ford had been painted black on top, then plain white in the middle. Then, as if an afterthought, some the leftover black paint was used on the bottom of the car. The black tires were painted with a wide white circle all around the outside of the tire, which I figured would show one and all that we kept even our tires clean. Dad said the white-circle tires were called "whitewall tires." Those tires carried us across half of the giant Texas highway map, then across the entire Louisiana and Mississippi highway maps, and finally across much of the last highway map, for a place called Alabama. These places with their individual highway maps were called states, not streets, my mama said.

When the black-and-white Fairlane slowed down on the asphalt highway, my heart was overjoyed with the idea of meeting our new family, the Anglo family that was new to my mother and me. We turned onto a red-orange dirt road. I hopped up to fold my skinny legs and kneel on the car's back seat so I could look out the back windshield. My arms laid flat and my hands overlapped on the back dashboard, which connected the car seat to the back windshield. Our whitewall wheels played with the dirt road, making red-orange clouds that swirled into the air and then faded into low branches of the tall pine trees that flanked the country road. I figured a country road meant only one car at a time could travel on the road. If two cars met, one of drivers had to politely pull over and let the other car pass. As they passed each other, the drivers smiled and waved a hand or tipped their hat or both. We rode a long time, about an hour. Feeling drowsy from the long summer drive and disoriented by the swirling orange cloud, I realized that my sense of time was completely confused. Finally, the car slowed – even for a country road. That's when I heard my dad say, "There's the fork in the road."

It was my clue that we were almost there. Sacrificing my orange cloud vigil, I hopped off my knees and spun around just in time to look ahead for the fork in the road. I had never seen a fork – or a spoon – in the road, nor did I understand *why a fork would even be in the road.* As hard as I looked *bueno pues nada*, nothing! Well, if there was a fork in the road, it wasn't very shiny. And it was surely too small for my eyes to see. All I saw, was a country road that had split to become two roads like open arms. We took the road to the left in the backward part of the country. We must have run over the fork, too.

I jumped back to the kneeling position on the car's back seat to get a rear view. The dusty red clouds were growing smaller. It was disappointing to never have seen the fork. I was anxious and turned around to sit on the edge of the car seat to look ahead once again.

The car slowed down on the sloping road. For the first time in all my life I saw a hill house. We passed a small hill in which a set of twin front doors had been built. I thought it was backward because most people live in a house *on* the hill not in a house *in* the hill. Alabama sure was confusing!

Just passed the hill house, our car coasted in front of an ancient family house that sat behind a small dirt parking area, the same color as the dirt road. The Fairlane rolled to a stop in front of a gray weathered wooden house lightly dusted with the Huntsville red road powder. The front screen door swung wide and two elders emerged to greet us. The old man opened his son's door while the old woman opened my mother's door. Stepping out of the Fairlane, Mama and I were introduced to our new Anglo family.

El viejecito, the old man, wore a Sunday shirt, khaki pants and what they called "spenders" to hold his pants up. The old woman wore a floral print dress. As was the custom then, she also wore a full apron of a different fabric edged with a sort of pretty squiggly edging that she said was "ric rac." My dad told me *los viejitos*, the elders, had salt-and-pepper hair, but still disappointed about the fork incident, I didn't even bother looking at their hair. My eyes just wandered off to the side. When I did look at them, I spotted the elders' wire-rimmed glasses. I was curious to know if they knew Benjamin Franklin personally. Oh my! Visions of my coloring poor old Mexican Benjamin Franklin came to my mind.

The woman was like *mi abuelita*, like my mother's mother in Texas. My mother said this was my new grandmother. Why, I wondered? I found the conversation upsetting. Why replace *mi abuelita* in Texas who I knew and loved. Mi *abuelita* loved me very much, too. There was no need to replace her. I did not understand. This lady seemed nice enough, but she was just a stranger who I all of a sudden had permission to talk to.

I had already tanned to my summer skin tone. It was dark cinnamon like other people in Alabama and not the same color as the Anglo woman or the Anglo man. Suddenly I wondered if things are all different in the backward part of the country, you know – backward. If so, my new grandmother would not love me all that much.

"*Abuelita?*" I asked in a tone that Tonto may have used upon first meeting the Lone Ranger. I looked into the lady's eyes, which were like two wet shiny gray pearls.

The elderly woman looked down at me, studying me and gently said.

"Call me ... Mamaw."

"Mamaw? *Así que, ¿qué es esto?* Mamaw?" I asked. "What is this Mamaw?"

"Yes, Mamaw," she confirmed. I wondered if she understood Spanish. I wondered what had changed the custom of calling grandmothers *abuelita* in this place quite a ways from Texas. I had to try to understand all the new ways - backward. I was instructed that my new grandfather was called "Papaw," not *Abuelito* like we said in Texas. It was confusing with these strangers who had become my "kinfolk by marriage," as they said with their Alabama accents, which were no match for my own Mexican accent (which was, of course, just being introduced to them).

Later that same day I got a new aunt called Helen. They also called her a teenager. A yellow school bus dropped her off at the dirt parking area by the house. I guessed it is what they did with teenagers in that part of the country. It took another day to finish meeting our other new kinfolks by marriage. But I met them all.

Another day I was playing with one of my kinfolk by marriage named Larry. He and I were making a small garden under a shade tree. The kinfolk always told me to play in the shade. I guessed they thought I would lighten up. But I could have told them it was not going to work - not even the cleanser made me lighten up! Anyway Larry and I were digging under the shade tree and decided to make a garden under the tree.

But then Larry said, "We ain't got no seeds." I didn't really understand what he meant, he had that Alabama accent, too. I wondered how he got it so young. He knew more about this than I did. I just knew about digging and planting *semillas*. He got up off the ground and ran toward Mamaw's house. I followed. Larry asked Mamaw for some seeds. Mamaw gave each of us a handful of corn seeds to plant. When I saw the seeds, they were what I knew as *semillas*.

Then Papaw said with his husky voice, "Them thar ahr

stiril."

Somehow when Mamaw sweetly said, "Sush naewe, Papaw" Papaw did.

We took the corn seeds and planted them in rows under the shade tree with its bulging roots. After Larry went home, I watered the seeds every day like Larry told me. It was a bright day when I looked up and saw Papaw. He was standing on the porch looking at me watering the corn seeds. He stood silently holding on to his "spenders" and shaking his head from side to side. The seeds were watered every day. Keep the faith, I thought. Mi Abuelita had taught me with her dichos, proverbs. I remembered the one, "Todo es posible con Dios delante de ti," "All is possible with God before you." Like the corn of my Mexican ancestral source of life and the wisdom of the Mexican faith healer of our neighborhood in San Antonio, my faith began to grow more with time. Then, tiny green leaves began to appear.

Finally Larry came back for a visit. We ran to check our garden under the shade tree. He squealed and went running to Mamaw and Papaw's house. He was all excited. In his squeaky voice, he called for Mamaw. When she came outside, Larry took her hand. Guessing that was what I was supposed to do, too, I took Mamaw's other hand. I had regressed to my "monkey-see, monkey-do" world. Larry led us to the small garden we had planted. Papaw hurried behind us. Larry squealed.

"Luck Mamaw. Luckit waat we grow'd."

A row of tiny green leaves quivered with the wind. Other sprouts were just breaking the surface of the ground. They were growing with a child's faith under the tree. (And yes, under a shady tree.) The elders were surprised with what they saw, but I wasn't. It's the way things happened there, all backward.

Besides, *mi abuelita* had taught me to also say a prayer when a *semilla*, a seed, is planted. She must have also known with me so far away from her I would be all right with the new family. She must have known children are like seeds, they will grow where and how you plant them.

There was a lot of excitement in Mamaw's house late one day. That afternoon, there was a lot of talk of "the tornado" coming. Everyone sat listening to the radio to know the "tornado's" whereabouts. The grownups were chattering, talking and whispering at different times about what they were going to do when the tornado arrived.

I sensed the strange excitement around me. No one, I mean *no one* had to get me excited about "the tornado" coming. I had never met "the tornado"; I wondered if I could sit on his lap, like Santa Claus at the department store. I wondered what he was going to bring me. Would he bring what I asked for? I was so excited that he was coming!

I bathed and slipped into a fairly new cotton dress – my pretty green princess dress was at *Abuelita's* house. I was wearing white ruffled socks and the shiny black Mary Janes that didn't eat my socks. *Mi mama*, my mother braided my waist-length, dark brown hair letting a ribbon-entwined braid hang down behind each ear, falling forward to mid-chest. Ready for company, I asked and was granted permission to stay up and wait for "the tornado." Things were different in Texas; we weren't allowed to stay up for Christmas or other special days. I perched on a creaky chair, pulled my dress over my bony knees, and crossed my skinny legs at my ankles. My legs dangled in front of the chair. My hands played with my braids. I waited, letting my skinny legs swing while the chair screeched its song.

Even when I shifted, the old chair screeched an ache. That chair creaked a lot worse than my squeaking shoes. Tiptoeing to the front screen door, I pressed my face against the dusty screen and peered out to see if "the tornado" was coming. *Nada*, nothing yet. The screen door left kisses of grid impressions on my forehead and the smell of the screen's dust made me sneeze.

I turned away to wait for "the tornado" on the old familiar noisy chair. Humpf! The old chair had disappeared! It was nowhere to be found. Where was I going to wait for "the tornado"? Where? Then ... I saw Papaw had walked back into the room. He offered me that special seat Mamaw called "Papaw's upholster'd char." The tapestry of his chair had pictures made right into it, and its cushion was softer than any other chair in the room. I glanced at Papaw and smiled. I took my place and sat at the edge of the cushion. My legs hung neatly from the chair, as each of my bony arms sprawled across the overstuffed arms of Papaw's chair. Papaw was so considerate to stand so I could use his throne – his upholstered chair. I felt like a barrio princess.

My folks and kinfolks listened for news of "the tornado's" progress on the radio. I was lost in thought, remembering that when the radio made crackling sounds, as it did now, Abuelita said it was "*enfermo con estático.*" She was no radio repair lady, but she knew it was "sick with static." I thought, if his social plans were broadcast on the radio, "the tornado" must be pretty important in the backward part of the country. Everyone in the house anticipated "the tornado's" arrival. Adults confided plans to one another. I was surprised that Mamaw didn't do any decorating. She didn't dig into the cupboard to bring out her fancy dishes either.

In Texas, there were joyful decorations when Santa Claus or *El Conejito*, the Easter Bunny, came. It seemed there were to be no colorful decorations for a *fiesta* in Alabama. We were going to the cellar when "the tornado" came. It is what I overheard them whisper.

"The cellar ... where is the cellar?" I asked.

Mamaw took me to her front screen door. She pointed to the hill house up the road.

"Thet thaar is the cellar, jist op the road a ways," she said. "Thet's whaar we're ah goin' wayen a tornada's a comin'." I mean no disrespect, but that's how she and the kinfolks sounded to me, as I tried to take in their Alabama accents.

I stared at the small front door of the hill house they called a "cellar" and thought ... that's very strange. Someone as important as "the tornado" is coming and my new kinfolks plan to leave a big wooden house to greet their visitor in a little dirt hill house. It sure seemed all backward to me. Maybe ... just maybe, the door in the side of the hill house was hiding a specially decorated room for a fiesta, a party room; at least that's what I was thinking.

In that part of Alabama, there were so many wonderful giant pine trees; they seemed to touch the heavens. The towering trees were the most beautiful trees I had ever seen, more beautiful than those at Christmas tree lots in San Antonio. Mamaw's house sat in the middle of this Christmas-pine-tree-scented world. So, it didn't take long for the day's darkness to fall on the gray weathered house. While Papaw turned off the house lights, Mamaw went around lighting her different kerosene lamps, which is what the kinfolks called them. Those kerosene lamps were smart lamps. They worked, even without electricity and without batteries. The warm glow from those glass and metal lamps was soft and calming in the darkness of our new kinfolk's house and reminded me of the warm glow of *Abuelita*'s religious altar candles with their wax scent. The elders and my parents were all given lamps. They paced around waiting for "the tornado" to come. They carried their smart lamps in the night just like lightning bugs.

As the evening wore on, I began to feel the strain of staying up past my bedtime. Yawning and stretching my arms, I realized that I was tired of waiting for "the tornado." Mamaw led me to her bed. She told my mother to let me sleep on Mamaw's bed with my shoes on.

"Ahhh," I gasped, *mi abuelita* in Texas would let me do that, too, when my mom was not there.

"What about 'the tornado'" – my question was directed to anyone listening.

"We'll wake ya wayen the tornada is a comin'," Mamaw said.

I figured I was too tired to ask or try to understand the what-fors and because-whys of what I was told to do. "The tornado" was coming ... and I was told to sleep with my clothes and shoes on! In Texas, when the Easter Bunny, Tooth Fairies or Santa Claus came, we slept in our night gowns. This, too, seemed all backward. Thinking maybe I was just misunderstanding local custom, I laid down on the quilt-draped bed and watched my new kinfolks wander from room to room like trapped lightning bugs ... until I fell asleep.

Thunder shook the wooden house. Lightning flashed on the big dresser mirror in the house bedroom where I awoke. Lightning lit up the thin lace curtains over the double-window. It was alarming and I was suddenly wide awake! *Mi mama* rushed in to get me.

"Is 'the tornado' here?" I asked as I jumped from Mamaw's bed to the safety of my mother's strong yet tender arms.

She was breathing rapidly and said, "*No mi hija*, 'the tornado' is coming."

Everyone huddled by the front door. Nobody wanted to miss the very first glimpse of our special guest. Lightning illuminated wind-shaken pine trees and broken limbs strewn around the dirt yard. I did not think it was a very good idea to go out on a night like this! Again, what I saw happening in Alabama seemed completely backward. In Texas, we stayed inside when rain and winds got strong.

The sounds of pine cones pelleting the house roof, then rolling off announced that something very powerful was waiting outside. The echoes of Mamaw's empty galvanized garbage can rolling away were heard by all. The garbage can's lid, as if the can's shield, clanged against the pier and beams beneath Mamaw's house. I wondered what goodness could there be waiting outside? I did not think it was a good idea to go out on a wild night like this! In Texas, we stayed inside when rain sounded like many angry birds stomping on Abuelita's house roof or when her empty galvanized garbage can rolled down the street stolen by wind *en el barrio*.

What kind of way was this to meet "the tornado?" Not a good idea – at all!

I had a keen eye on how things happened in Huntsville,

Alabama. Things were truly different there in the Alabama night.

Papaw led Mamaw, who led the rest of us out of the safety of her warm home. Mamaw had a tight fist on the kerosene lamp and with her free hand she held her teenager's hand. Then, it was *mi mama's* turn. Carrying a lamp in one hand, she wrapped her free arm tightly around my shivering skinny shoulder. She held me close by her side when we stepped into the black night with its smell of moist red Alabama earth. The fierce wind and gritty sandy dirt wrapped themselves all around us and the kinfolks. The wind stung my eyes shut. I heard tree limbs breaking, tree branches rustling and the tall pine trees creaking. The sandy grit pinned and needled my skinny legs to dance. I cupped my trembling hand over my eyes while I glimpsed to the side to peek at "the tornado." Instead, I saw Papaw shrugging the wind as he leaned into it until he reached a big round post in the parking area. Mamaw and Helen bowed their bodies into the intense swirling wind also. The angry wind demanded respect and gave no choice to anyone or thing in its path. Mother and I submitted and bowed into it, too.

"Ya jest caint hep et, jest caint hep et," Mamaw yelled above the meanness of the harsh whistling wind in the terrifying night.

I thought that "the tornado" better be pretty important and bring me something very special now that we were going to meet it. I looked back. Dad was holding his lamp, his pant legs flapping like flags in the wind.

Papaw did something with a lever on a gray box mounted on the big pole. Then he rejoined the family march toward the cellar.

Mamaw started running and we followed. She opened the cellar door and led us all into the cellar. The faded glow from a lamp faintly lit the room with disappointment. The one-room house had walls made of dirt, lined with shelves made of aged raw lumber. It was like a scary house at Halloween. Spider webs hung like veils over jars of peach preserves, pickled beets, sweet butter pickles, apple butter and okra. The thin lacy webs also hung from shelf to shelf.

Another lamp sat on top of an old wooden barrel, beside a white pottery jug with a cork in it. The last one in, Papaw strained against the wind to close the rotten door, which squeaked as if it was straining just as much as Papaw's old-man muscles. Once he had the door closed, Papaw latched it as tight as he could. I watched his eyes flash quickly to the jug with the cork in it. Then he glanced at Mamaw, as if to ask her a question, though he did not speak. Mamaw glared at him; unspoken words conveyed her thought, "Don't ja' e'ven thank 'bout it!"

Somebody backed me into a dark corner where light from the lamps was blocked by the elders' bodies. I was afraid of the dark. Papaw warned me there might be field mice in the dark. There might be spiders under the shelves! I reconsidered "the tornado" and decided his visit was *not that important for me to be there with spiders, mice and other creepy crawlies in a dark scary corner of a dirt house!* A whimper escaped my lips. Suddenly, *mi mama* placed her lamp closer to me. I turned in its flickering light and saw – just inches from my nose – a big spider dancing on a giant vibrating web. The black spider pranced with legs that moved like Tom, the cat, when he was about to pounce upon Jerry, the mouse in the drive-in movie cartoons. A ragged whimper started down in my throat. By the time it rose to my mouth, the whimper had turned into a scream. I was sure that, even in spite of the howling wind outside the cellar door, "the tornado" had heard me. My mother squeezed me tightly to her hip while tightening her grip on the lamp in her other hand. Looking up, I saw Mamaw make her way through the crowded cellar – she and Pawpaw stood between the cellar door and my mother and me – to come to my aid. In her facial wrinkles I saw serious anger. She raised her slight old lady's arm to make a circle around the spider web's outer rim, held it like a penny candy sack from her hand, and – with a flick of the wrist, tossed it away from me. My Mamaw had no fear!

The wooden door shook faster and louder than I did. It was not fair; I was the smallest one there and I felt the biggest fear. There was a big rumble that sounded like thunder.

"What's that?" I shouted to be heard in the din.

"The tornada, I thank." Papaw hollered back.

Peach preserves with spiders? This was not a very appetizing way to host "the tornado." I was sure it was why Papaw was guarding the door and didn't let "the tornado" in the cellar. The wind began to simmer down. Rain pelted the door, sounding like hail. Lightning flashed through the door planks. The rumbling thunder finally stopped, but the fast-paced beating of my heart did not.

After almost all noises stopped, Papaw opened the cellar door and peeked outside. Lightning flashed again. Papaw looked ahead.

"Haus is thaar," Papaw said. That seemed to be the end of Papaw's curiosity. Papaw said he saw broken tree limbs and other piney wood debris on the road and warned us to walk carefully. We stepped out carefully, watching where we put our feet down, and watching for unsettled slithering snakes, we headed down the sloping road, away from where the fork was supposed to be in the road. Maybe the wind with its fury had taken the fork.

We were headed toward Mamaw's and Papaw's house. Papaw went to the gray metal box on the tall pole.

"Where's the tornado?" I asked feeling the words make me shiver.

Mamaw put her warm arm around me as we walked. Guiding me to her home. Come morning, all of us could see how well the tornado's friend, the rain, had given Mamaw a fresh-washed home. She spoke ever so simply. "The tornada 'as done gawn bye-bye, honey."

Then Papaw repeated, "Done gawn bye-bye."

I didn't get to see what I had been waiting much of the night for. Another disappointment! Again!

On that unpredictable night in Alabama, I learned that anticipating a tornado is not like preparing for a visit from the Easter Bunny, the Tooth Fairies or Santa Claus. A tornado brings the opposite kind of expectation. It brings terrible news, very scary mean weather stuff. It means even old people cannot be sure what to expect.

We were spared that tornado's destruction. Instead of pulling Mamaw's house up by its family roots, as it did to many down the road, the storm strengthened the bonds of our diverse family, which now included new kinfolks, in the little hill house they called a cellar. I realized grandmothers are all the same – rotund. A grandmother is full of love, whether she is called *Abuelita* or Mamaw. A grandmother has a special touch, often very gentle, yet can be tough when her grandchildren are in danger.

There was nothing backward about it. That first encounter with a tornado brought me something special, a place in Mamaw's circle of love. Yes, I found new love and security from kinfolks in the place my dad called, "the backward part of the country," the place he sometimes called Huntsville, Alabama.

All the same, it was "quite a ways from Texas."

VIII
The Big Chief and the Match Box

Psychological studies reveal that the 1950s are remembered by many with fondness and serenity. I remember the 1950s as a time that was simple, safe and happy. At East Ward Elementary, in Mrs. Stanley's third-grade class, I met the guy I was going to marry. It was the first time "marrying" came into my thoughts. What did marrying mean to me in the third grade? First, I had to find a guy I wanted to have fun with, share my days with. Once I found that guy, then he was the one to marry ... or at least it's what I thought marrying was all about. I figured it was as simple as that.

I learned about puppy love in the third grade. Puppy love meant having special feelings for someone who was not a family member. The essence of puppy love was in the air, along with the scents of swirled pencil shavings and pulverized lead. Young love! Penciled love notes circled the classroom. Momentous events were heightened by the gravity of new passions. Unanticipated events led my circle of friends to the

Big Chief and a match box.

Mrs. Stanley studied our flaming red writing tablets, their bonded edges frayed and corners curling. She guessed her students were earnestly applying themselves. And she was right. Tender young hearts scribbled pages of messages. Yes, the air of that third-grade classroom was charged with learning ... about first romance, young love. Folded messages were scattered among penmanship exercises, times tables and spelling lists under the lids of our desks. We passed love notes to each other in class, in hallway lines, in the cafeteria and at recess. Love notes navigated from the soft hands of one student and ebbed and flowed undetected to another until the loving note reached the blushing intended. Sixteen sweaty palms surreptitiously, masterfully maneuvered syrupy musings from seat to seat.

Yes, eight of us formed kind of an emotional exploration club. We sat near each other in class and played together at recess. There were four boys: Dion, Wesley, Steven and Davy. Perhaps not coincidentally, there were also four young girls: Pam, Patricia, my best friend Claudia ... and me. *I was different.* Our school had very few Mexican-American children. Those who were there mostly came from the low-income housing development where my family lived. (Later generations of families called the development "the Bricks.") My school friends were Anglos. Even so, I felt accepted by them as a friend.

As soon as Mrs. Stanley released us for recess, as if by magnetic force, we gravitated into a group. Once formed, the circle broke. We ran, dashed and skipped toward the playground merry-go-round. It was a Wellington playground merry-go-round with six metal handle bars welded to a metal disk about six feet in diameter. We girls mounted the merry-go-round first and held on tight to the handle bars. The boys pushed the merry-go-round with their big third-grade muscles, then stood by and watched us as we spun around in circles. We were four giggling girls. Round and round on the merry-go-round we flew. Hair curls, strands and braids in shades of blonde, strawberry blonde, brown and dark brown were whooshed away from our laughing faces by the momentum of each rotation. Each turn made us giggle, each time a little more. We girls stretched out our skinny little arms and gently touched fingertips with the boys as we circled. Once in a while the boys grabbed the steel handle bars of the merry-go-round, ran alongside the rotating disk, and then jumped on the merry-go-round for the ride, too. Our circle of friends was very united.

Wesley and Patricia were each blonde with beautiful blue eyes. They were the very definition of puppy love to the rest of us. Wesley and Patricia were inseparable – in the third grade! They gazed at one another with owl eyes and goofy expressions. They held hands when the chatting teachers were not looking. This was serious!

Davy was my friend. We were near each other often. He was a little taller than I was (everyone was taller than I was!). He had brown hair styled in what the boys called a crew cut in those days. I suspected that he combed his hair with Brylcreem hair cream, which we saw advertised on TV. The jingle was "Brylcreem a little dab'll do ya! Bryclcreem you look so debonair ..." Davy didn't need any dabs, he was "pretty good fine" as he was.

Once, Davy fell off the merry-go-round. Actually, I was not sure if he lost his balance or if he was just a little bit awkward like the rest of us. Anyway, he fell off the spinning metal disk. I saw him let go of the handle bar and off he went. The merry-go-round's centrifugal force sent him flying away just as a spinning yo-yo whirls away from the string. As he stumbled, his arms waved wildly. He was trying to avoid a painful impact. But it was painfully late. His head hit the hot playground asphalt, mouth first. His lip didn't stand a chance against pavement; it split his lip open. As his lip began to bleed, Davy began to cry.

If his lip would have split any further, he probably could have played two harmonicas at once! It was the first time we saw a split-lip accident on the playground. Usually we saw scraped scrawny knees or skinned playground-dirtied hands.

Teachers and the playground safety patrol surrounded Davy. They knelt next to him, as if he was an injured prince. When the worst of the bleeding stopped, they helped him into the school to the nurse's room. Davy didn't return to recess. My dear friend was hurt. Tears trickled from my brown eyes, slowly down my cheeks. My worry worsened when Davy didn't return to Mrs. Stanley's class after recess. I saw worry in our friends' faces. Even though our teacher told us Davy was being cared for by the school nurse, I was uneasy. My brain just would not focus on class work and I cried quietly at my desk. I remembered a time in San Antonio when my cousins and I saw someone leave the *barrio* in an ambulance, probably being taken to the emergency room. Back then, we asked each other if the injured person was going to die. Now in school, the same troubling thoughts flashed back and overwhelmed my young brain. That night before bed, I said a small prayer for Davy.

Davy did not die. The next day, he returned to school. At morning recess, Davy explained to our circle of friends what had happened to him. Falling on his mouth, he had a chipped a tooth. The school principal had called his parents who had taken Davy to the family dentist.

At home, I often talked about Davy. I talked about Davy being the best pal anyone could have and about Davy pushing the merry-go-round faster than anyone else. Besides, Davy returned to school after his playground accident, proving that he was a valiant one, *el valiente.*

I shared with my mom the school-day events on the playground with Davy and our friends. One day as I talked with my mom, she interrupted me and asked, "Who is this Davy who you talk so much about?"

I guess she expected me to say Davy Lopez or Davy Rodriquez or maybe Davy Montez. There were no such boys in our school, but I guessed she was expecting a Davy with a Mexican surname. I was so sure Davy was a friend to share fun and life with. The playground experience was proof that my vision was true and there was nothing to worry about. That is all one needed to marry in my third-grade mind and heart. So with that, my answer to my mother was pure and simple. "He's the boy I'm going to marry someday, Mom. His name is Davy Brown."

"Davy Brown!" she exclaimed, chuckling an approving smile. "I know him!"

"You do?" I asked, both curious and surprised. I don't know why I was surprised, since ours was a small town. But curious is what I did well.

"Yes. He is my boss' son," she replied.

My mother worked in a meat market. Her boss, Mr. Brown, was a prominent businessman and civic leader in our community. He owned a small grocery store and a small car dealership and he came from strong family roots.

Although society was beginning to accept interracial marriages, society was not ready to accept business owners or professionals crossing boundaries by marrying "hired help" or someone who lived in low-income housing. Cultural differences were a slanderous concern. I had begun to realize social boundaries like those I experienced at Ira Ogden Elementary in San Antonio. Now, as a small-town third-grader, I was learning more about boundaries everywhere we went.

My little third-grade Mexican-bred heart was broken and sad, sensing the prospects for romance were limited in ways I had not expected. That night, I cried myself to sleep. I saw Davy's warm smile fading away in my dreams. The reality was that I was experiencing a puppy love broken heart for the first time. I would never be able to marry Davy.

The next day I was unexplainably cool to Davy. Knowing what I knew about boundaries, I needed to downplay any romantic feelings, if this is what they truly were, between us. Even in the third grade, I knew it was not his fault. Davy never learned why I began to shy away from him.

But thanks to Patricia and Wesley, my timing was a little off. Wesley and Patricia had openly decided they would marry someday. But until then, they were going to say their elementary school wedding vows during recess. The rest of us were to serve as witnesses. I did not understand what it meant to be witnesses, only that we were all meeting behind one of the school classroom wings for the third-grade wedding. I guessed it was what witnesses did. The eight of us were such third-grade romantics.

Somebody who knew more about weddings wrote vows, declaring a lifetime commitment. In our third-grade minds, a lifetime meant until we reached our twelfth grade, our senior year in high school. Claudia made the third-grade "diamond" rings. My job was to bring a jewelry case for the rings.

Finally, the wedding day came. It was set for the morning recess. When Mrs. Stanley released us for recess, we gravitated to our circle of friends. This time instead of making our way to the merry-go-round, we all ran, dashed and skipped behind one of the school classroom wings, where it was more quiet and private. Once there, we all stood in a circle and gave each other the "now what do we do?" look. Having no idea what to do next, I looked up, seeing the bright blue sky, white tender clouds, and the warm golden sun. The sun – then as now – was a symbol of hope, faith and love. I closed my dreamy eyes; my bronzed face felt the sun's warmth.

The vows of eternal love were spoken as Wesley and Patricia held hands tenderly. Then, it was time for the wedding rings. Claudia and I had met in the playground before school. Claudia put the third-grade craft-made rings into a box, decorated with the same design as the rings. I opened the ring case gently. It was actually an empty penny match box into which I had stuffed a thin layer of aspirin bottle cotton. Secretly, I hoped mother would not miss the cotton, which I hoped would make the rings seem more real. The "diamond" rings that Wesley and Patricia exchanged were made from a pulp strip of a Big Chief tablet with number two lead-colored "gems." Standard elementary white paste bonded the paper strip rings. Even as third-graders, we knew the pretend diamond rings made from tablet paper were less enduring than the puppy love bond Patricia and Wesley shared. After the "wedding," we celebrated by going to our favorite recess spot, the playground merry-go-round.

The next school year took me to another school across town and away from my third-grade friends. Years later I saw them again in junior high school, where Davy and I greeted each other once in a while. I was so shy that I hardly ever spoke to Dion and Steven. Wesley attended another junior high on the other side of town, within blocks from the East Ward Elementary. The other third-grade girls had all moved away – all except me. It was time for me to become friends with people of my own heritage and culture, respecting cultural boundaries.

In my freshman year of junior high school, my dad's U.S. Army duty took us to Germany, a European country with its own culture and language. Schwäbisch Gmünd, Germany, was very charming and set in a valley between two low mountains, which, in Texas, we called hills.

We lived at the top of one hill where all the American citizens lived as a community. I and many of my circle of friends from that community shared many playful, joyful rides on sleds. When our hill was snow draped, we used wooden, German-made sleds, toboggans and galvanized garbage can lids to slide down the memorable hill. We, and others who came after us, simply called it "the Hill."

After years of being with my new friends in Germany, one by one our dads' tour of duty rotation came due.

At last we returned to the United States for my senior year of high school. Once again I saw what was left of my third-grade circle of friends: Dion, Steven, Wesley and Davy. We were all in the high school band, where I played the flute. We had joined the high school band – "the Marching 100." Dion and Davy played the trumpet or cornet. Wesley played the saxophone. Steven, who played the oboe, had the biggest smile and most joyful disposition. Dion, Davy, Wesley and I were on the quiet side. I thought Dion was the brightest of us all.

Although we recognized each other, we rarely spoke to each other but we did greet one another occasionally. I was already dating the boy I would ultimately marry. Andres' heritage is Mexican. Andres lived within an hour from where I lived. He was gregarious and a recognized athlete. He participated in high school football, basketball and track and lettered in each. In school, he was called Andrew or Andy, depending on which gender or teacher was addressing him. He was a loyal stinging Bumble Bee from Academy High and a graduate among the class hive of twenty-six Bumble Bees. I tried really hard to overcome my Mexican accent. In younger years it was often ridiculed. My strategy was "no spoken words, no ridicule."

Mother encouraged me to socialize in high school, but my comfort zone was in a book, a movie or practicing on my flute. The less I spoke the more comfortable I was. I was very shy until I met Andres.

After high school graduation, my third-grade circle

of friends went separate ways on their life journeys. Dion's scholastic aptitudes led him to college opportunities. Stephen, Davy and Wesley also began college.

The Cowhouse Hotel was the newest, grandest hotel in our town, luxurious for its time. I worked as a budding bus girl for a year before I began my studies at the new junior college at the edge of the Bell County line, just outside of Killeen. Central Texas College was the Cinderella story of the year according to a national TV station. The college was projected to have about a two hundred-student enrollment, but instead had about two thousand students under the leadership of the college president, Luis Morton, who by the way was also of Mexican heritage.

My last college work-study assignment was at the USO, where I met many young men coming from or going to Vietnam. Many shared their plans for weddings before they left or when they returned. There were daily visits from many handsome young men with hopeful dreams of happy futures. Andres proposed shortly after I began working at the USO. Prayers were said for many young men and fellow classmates.

Vietnam was on the television news every night. I hardly watched the news. Watching horrid images of terrified boys made me sad. They had to put education, romance, everything on hold until their military service was fulfilled – and that was *if* they lived. The Vietnam War was still in the news headlines when Andres and I married. We put college on hold. We took control of our married life by his volunteering for a tour of duty in lieu of the uncertainty of waiting for the draft. By luck of the draw, when a son was the only or last to carry the family name to the next generation, he seldom went to Vietnam. Private

Samarripa was ordered to serve in a special unit in Hawaii.

The fragrance of fresh pineapple juice welcomed me when I arrived a month later as an Army wife. I missed the turberose, carnation and orchid leis on my arrival. All the sightseeing was completed in one day on the island of Oahu. Not much to do on the island of paradise. All our children were born in the short years of paradise life and hula hula. They were born at Tripler Army Medical Hospital in Honolulu, Oahu, Hawaii. At each blessings or baptism, our priest said, "Free set of china with the tenth child!" Our parents offered to buy us china!

We managed apartments. The jobs allowed us unexpected opportunities to save for funding college studies upon our return to the mainland. When we returned to Killeen, we each pursued college degrees.

With my first classes came an unexplainable shock. Our return to Killeen had brought a return of my old reclusive habits from high school days. On several occasions, I did not go into any grocery store if I saw anyone I knew in the parking lot. One day, after waiting for almost two hours in the car with my babies, I decided that living with painful shyness was not fair to them. I had to resolve the painfully introverted habits that controlled me – painful because my children were affected in the disturbing routine. In this difficult time, my grandmother's deep-seated faith helped me to overcome my demons. Then I remembered *mi abuelita's dicho-todo es posible con dios adelante,* all is possible with God before you. So often when she saw me hesitate about anything, she expressed everlasting encouraging words, the same words that echoed in my mind and enforced my conviction to overcome any obstacle. The words, which unleashed inner strength to carry me through this and other fears, were *Si, se puede ... si, se puede.* Her strong words whispering in my head, *yes, you can ... yes, you can.* It was not Barack Obama who coined this phrase. The phrase was active in our Mexican culture long before he used it as a campaign slogan. The memory of my *abuelita's* faith and wisdom set me on the course to overcome my reclusive instincts. After a period of struggle – perhaps four months – I was freed from the old demons. Grateful for myself, my husband and my children, I was able to resume a happy and fearless life.

In the middle of a day, I went shopping at my neighborhood grocery store. My shopping cart appeared as if I had just chosen and carefully placed into my cart the three loveliest babies under three years old off the grocery store shelf. The shopping cart looked like a baby stroller and as such I headed to the baby food aisle. Usually, it was easy to find the aisle with the varied baby cries, but not that day, a slow, quiet business day in the store.

My eyes squinted to peruse all the baby food jar labels with their palettes of pureed yellow, orange, red and green vegetables. I talked softly to my babies, just like a motherly waitress.

"Wooould yoooooooou like ... pebbly peas, smushy squash, crushy carrots, ooooh blah blah, beets?!" They giggled but never answered. I laughed with them and dared not ask them again too loudly with such silliness.

The silly shopping requests stopped; it was time to carefully begin selecting jars. The dull clatter of glass baby jars for varied ages made for a crowded cart. When I tried to make room for more jars amongst the chubby babies, I caught a glimpse of a tall young man sweeping the baby food aisle down by the refrigerated foods department. I completed my selection of baby food, careful to keep my cart out of his way.

As the young man's chore brought him closer, I looked up and saw that it was Davy. There he was – the hired help – in his dad's store. I froze. My mouth hung open while I stared in shock. As we would say in third grade, I gaped as if "waiting to catch flies." When he turned and recognized me, the moment was both awkward yet somehow pleasant, a welcome surprise. We had a succinct chat. His familiar soft smile had not lost its charm. Half-embarrassed, I nervously returned his smile – briefly – before looking away. I did not see any tell-tale signs of a chipped tooth, but then again, when it's a special prince like Davy, who notices?

Adjusting my squirming baby, I looked up at Davy. He was leaning against the broom handle, like a shepherd against his staff. Davy's eyes gave an elusive, questioning glance at my shopping cart. I looked at him and proudly affirmed, "Yes, they are all mine."

He chuckled and smiled again, and then said he had to get back to his chore and we bid our mature farewells. Slowly, my cart seemed to roll itself forward. The fading sounds of the broom's *whoosh* continued behind me. I pushed the reality cart forward, but the flashback of memories circled in my mind like a playground merry-go-around. The coolness coming from the dairy foods cases ahead brought me back to my grocery list. It was written on notebook paper, not from a Big Chief tablet. My pace hastened as the rattling of baby food jars and the pleas of my babies joyfully wailing a soft, "weeeeeooo," rose with my pace. I made my way to the milk, butter and eggs.

Years later, I read about Davy in the society section of our Killeen newspaper. He and his wife were celebrating a benchmark anniversary. When mother ran her errands in town, occasionally she ran into Davy and reported my life events as he listened politely. When my mother volunteered her version of their conversation, I scolded her in embarrassment. "Mother, please do not inform him about me, he is a busy man."

Mother's fractured defense was, "Well, sometimes he asks."

Even at that time, I regretted my bashfulness, my guarding social boundaries in a way that may have disrespected or hurt my old friend's loyalty and friendship. Decades later, I ran into Davy again when my mom, Davy's dad and Davy himself helped me buy a new (used) car. Davy and I had been missing each other at the dealership, until – during the holidays – I finally got a chance to visit him during my hometown visit to the folks. I thanked him for his help and friendship. We caught up on our families and our children. Our senior class picture hung on his office wall. Davy had become his dad, a prominent businessman. As we chatted, we paused to reflect. With our lifetime of wisdom, what should we have done differently? We agreed that we should have gotten more education and made more of an effort to shed our inbred timidity. The visit ended warmly and innocently – just like our third-grade friendship.

I recall a 1956 song sung by Doris Day. The chorus went, "*Que sera, sera,* Whatever will be, will be. The future's not ours to see. *Que sera, sera,* what will be, will be."

The decade of the 1950s was a simple, safe and happy time. It was East Ward Elementary, Mrs. Stanley's third-grade class where among scents of swirled pencil shavings and pulverized lead I met the boy I thought I was going to marry. It was a happy time to experience puppy love through a Big Chief and a match box.

The author's mother, Lupe Barron McNeir (at left), with her co-worker and friend, Carmen Fragrosa, at their workplace on Kelly AFB, Texas, about 1945.

IX

My Pre-owned Dog, Ring

The whitewall tires of the 1953 Oldsmobile rolled up the inclined driveway. The Oldsmobile, which we simply called the Olds, had a fern green color on the lower body and the car's top was a creamy white. Mother loved that Olds, and seemed not to notice the brakes squeaking as the wheels rolled to a stop.

I remember hearing a dog's angry barking above the high-pitched squeaking brakes. Mother and I sat in the car waiting. We eyed at each other half-way for a long moment, delighting in our love, in our appreciation for that big car, and for the excitement of arriving at a new home. Yet, we saw the mutual dread in each other's eyes when we turned to look at one another because of that barking. Mom reassured me it was safe; the dog was in the fenced yard. Mother got out to unlock the back door of the house. It was my turn to climb out of the car, and I ran to her side. She opened the back door to our "new home."

My parents' hard work had paid off. Finally we were moving from low-income housing projects to our "new" home clear across our small town. We were moving to the other side of the railroad tracks! The single-story frame house was pre-prefab and pre-owned, but it was now *our* home.

"Oh Mother, it is nice and *clean*." My soft voice echoed through the empty the house. It was so exciting to be in our very own home. The echoes gave me the giggles then Mother's laughter echoed in the house, too.

The echo of my giggles seemed to run ahead of me as I searched from room to room, scouting for *my* room. Mother said the bedroom nearest the front door would be mine. An open floor plan meant that the living room, dining room and kitchen were all open in one area. My joyful laughter was uncontrollable when I stood in the middle of the living area owning all that space.

Then Mother gave me the news. "Sgt. Parrot left you a present in the backyard." Standing by the door of the empty room, Mother knew her words would resonate past where the dining table would later stand and into the family room area.

"What? Sgt. Parrot *left me* a present?"

I met Sgt. and Mrs. Parrot when they gave us the initial house tour. I recalled him standing in the middle of the living room, serious in his military stance. He wore his olive drab green U.S. Army fatigue pants, which ballooned at the bottom so the pants covered the top of his eight-inch, spit-shined black leather boots. Sgt. Parrot was proud of those boots and I was impressed. I was even more impressed by the white T-shirt, tucked into his pants so emphatically taunt. His arms were battle ready, muscular and fit; his hands rested on his hips.

Even his sharply trimmed crew cut hair stood at attention in the Army style of the era. All business, there was no smile on his face.

"Go see." Mom pointed to the backyard.

The barking started again the moment I opened the front door, though the dog was nowhere in sight. Cautiously, I entered the backyard, seeing a triple-door commercial refrigerator between me and where the dog's barking sounds came from. It was a great place for the refrigerator, between the dog and me. On tiptoe, I snuck around the refrigerator. Keeping my distance, I leaned around the corner to sneak a peek at the dog. He snarled, bared his teeth, and strained against his chain. After an especially ferocious growl, I began backing away.

Then my eyes fell upon the present Mother was talking about. At least I hoped it was.

Leaning against the back wall of the house was a bicycle, its faded royal blue fenders slightly splattered with rust spots. Both tires were present – though one was flat. With a little oil, the chain would be as good as new. The few rusty spots on the fenders and frame did not dishearten me a bit. All *my bike* needed was a good washing, a little car wax, air in the flat tire and some oil. It would be good as new!

Excited, I danced and ran inside to tell my mother.

"There's a bike in the backyard!"

"Yes, I know. Sgt. Parrot wanted you to have it," she said.

"There's a dog in the backyard, too." Still fearful, I mentioned my other backyard discovery.

"Yes, the dog is yours, too. Sgt. Parrot left him for you. His name is Ring," Mother said.

"Why?" I asked curiously. "Why did he do that?"

Mother explained that Sgt. Parrot's daughter did not need the bike anymore, and he wanted to leave the dog because he thought it would be good for me. Sometimes children need a pet, he had told Mother. Since Sgt. Parrot knew we had lived in apartments, he knew I did not own a dog.

So, I lived in a pre-fabricated, pre-owned house, with a pre-owned bicycle and a pre-owned dog, whose pet-friendliness was definitely in question.

Joy was replaced in my mind with worries of responsibility for *my new bike* and a fang-baring dog. It was too much for a girl to take in quickly.

Where to start assimilating all of the new developments?

Would Mother let me ride the bicycle to school? She said no. For my information, she said I would complete my third-grade year at my old school, clear across town.

I returned gingerly to the yard to consider Ring.

Ring looked like Lassie from the television show by the same name. Ring was a bit smaller and did not have as many liberties as Lassie did. Ring was tied to an anchor in the ground with a chain. Pencil-thick links kept him in place. He barked a lot, often growling and showing his teeth. I was tempted to lean in and show him my teeth, but I decided against it.

Sgt. Parrot had made a dog house and left it behind, too. It was just the right size for Ring. The dog house, sided and roofed the same as the house, stood in front of the walk-in refrigerator, from which the doors had been removed. The huge ice box had been there some time under the Texas sun, its paint now a dull, powdery white. I guessed it was there to block the wind and to shade the dog house. Ring was fed from a white enamelware porcelain wash pan with a red-trimmed rim. The pan was wide and hand deep; Ring's food "bowl" was left behind, too. A second wash pan of the same size and same style served as his water "bowl."

Mother began to save table scraps for Ring in an old sauce pan with a short handle. My first time feeding Ring was frightening. Both of my hands gripped tightly on the handle of the heavy sauce pan, as I carried Ring's food outside. Seeing me, Ring lunged toward me, stirring up dust and growling ferociously. The chain to which he was anchored suddenly seemed insufficient! I imagined Ring mauling me if that chain broke. The chain link gate, its diamond-shaped links waving like a flag in a stiff breeze, was the only thing between those giant dog teeth and little ole cinnamon-colored me.

Aside from that gate, there was nothing between the back door and those monster dog teeth. Nothing! He barked nonstop and strained every muscle trying to reach me. Ring made his stand between his food bowl and me. His food bowl was too far away for me to venture inside the gate. Quite frankly *any distance* was too far for me to venture past that gate, which remained closed as I assessed my shrinking lifespan.

The sauce pan was getting heavier. I plunked it on the ground, before sitting on the doorstep to ponder my task and its risks. The word "dilemma" suddenly made sense to me. It was wearisome thinking and besides it was better to wait inside the house. I rose to go inside. The garden water hose caught my attention. It was a good substitute for a rope; it was the only thing around from which I figured I could make a lasso. I utilized a galvanized bucket found nearby, turning the bucket upside down by the gate to give me a bit more height. I grabbed my make-do lasso and began to whirl it.

"Whoop, whoop, whoop," the lasso droned overhead.

"Whoop, whoop, whoop."

My aim was set. I tossed the lasso and missed. Our Girl Scout leaders did not teach us how to lasso in Brownies but I *had to try* just like the Lone Ranger. My next attempt was to use the single jump rope lasso loop. The garden hose was shaped like a horse shoe, like the letter U.

Ring barked constantly during my "lasso the food pan" attempts; there were many tries. Finally the hoop caught the empty food bowl. A slow gentle pull was all that was needed to drag the tub closer to me until it was next to the gate. I jumped off the bucket, picked up the sauce pan to dump it over the gate and into the tub. My wrists wiggled from the sauce pan's weight. I bit my lip to muster strength to get the pan over the gate. Finally ... bull's-eye! The food was in Ring's bowl.

Just one problem: Ring's chain didn't stretch far enough for him to reach the bowl now that it was next to the gate. The floor mop was handy. From outside the gate, I used the mop to push the food bowl within Ring's reach. As he began to eat, Ring could not help stealing glances at me, his beautiful amber-tinted eyes betraying his anxiety. I turned on the water and used the water hose to spike fresh water into Ring's water bowl. Ring had food and water.

After that, Ring's food pan stayed near the gate. Since, due to knotting at the stake, the reach of Ring's heavy tow chain was different every day. So every day I had a new challenge to feed and water Ring. He continued to bark a great deal. Why?

I wondered.

I tried watching morning television programs one Saturday while Mom was at work. It was hopeless. Ring was barking so loud. Annoyed, I started hollering, too. Once, I shouted angrily, "Ring, be quiet! Be quiet, Ring! Hush up, Ring!" My hollering had no effect. The dog barked on. He was an angry dog for sure. At last his barking faded, until finally it stopped.

The quiet was strange. It was too quiet. I had to investigate.

Ring was in the most frightening position. He had looped the heavy chain around his dog house. Then in some freakish way, as he encircled his dog house, his body became trapped in chain loops. One of the loops bound around his neck. Another loop pinned his legs. His lovely hazel eyes were bulging from their eye sockets. I was terrified seeing him so helpless. His eyes told me that he, too, was terrified.

His panting shallow and his tongue hung loosely from his mouth.

What a frightening way to see a living being!

How can any of God's creatures have another of God's creatures chained in such an oppressing way? Why?

Almost on its own, and very slowly, my hand opened the gate latch. I stepped inside Ring's domain. The gate stood ajar, just in case I needed to turn and run. Ring did not bark. Pitifully, his eyes locked on me. I inched another step closer to him. He shifted, but was locked in the chain. My steps froze. My heart pretty near stopped.

"Hi there, Ring." I greeted him softly.

"Hi there, Ring. Hi there, Ring." Softly, I spoke to him in his nest of coiled chain. I repeated the greeting with each step, closer ... closer to him.

"Steady," I told myself, until I was close enough to touch him. But my hand, at first, wouldn't reach out to the dog that had scared me for so long. Then, as if I had no control over it, my shaking hand reached out to touch his head. I stroked the hair between his ears. I was amazed when my hand appeared under his jaw with all fingers intact.

"There ... there, boy." Softly repeated, my gentle words seemed to meet Ring's beautiful eyes, which were locked on me.

Reaching slowly around his tail, I was able to remove one loop of chain from his hind legs. It seemed a good place to start: no teeth there. Then slowly, I leaned over the dog house to dislodge a loop of chain. Ring struggled to free himself, but his front legs and head were still bound. I unwound the chain from his front legs, then his neck. His breathing came a little easier. I whispered to him, tenderly speaking his name. I stroked his fur, dirt-dusted shades of earth yellow, ochre and fawn.

When I stroked his neck, I noticed a white ring of fur around his neck. The white ring was his marking! That's where he got his name, I concluded. The realization came to me so much like a lightning bolt, I was surprised Ring hadn't become alarmed. But of course, it had happened inside my head, silently.

"Ring," I said to myself, with a new sense of wonder. His eyes softened when I said his name then.

It only took a short while to finish untangling him. He was cooperative, quiet and more importantly, he was not trying to bite. I realized that, for the first time, his teeth were not bared. At last, tentative as a newborn, he stood on his own. Ring limped to his water bowl. As he lapped water, his eyes softened as they tracked my retreat to the gate. There was no more barking.

I closed the gate, sighed, and slowly walked to the back door. Things might be different with Ring now, I hoped.

I decided to speak to Mom on Ring's behalf.

Mom first heard what had happened to Ring when she came home from work. I pleaded with her to try using a cotton cord instead of the heavy tow chain. Mother said she would think about it. The next day, I entered Ring's domain cautiously, stepping carefully. First, I tied the cotton cord to his collar; next I tied the cord to the anchor. Finally, I unhooked the heavy chain. Ring seemed to like the lightweight cord.

The cord worked pretty great ... until the next school day. Mom was driving me to school, when suddenly she gasped, looking into the rear view mirror.

"What's wrong?" I asked.

"Ring ... is following us!" she exclaimed.

"What?" I hopped on the seat to look back. Lassie would have been proud of Ring as he ran behind our car. "How did he get loose?"

"I don't know!" My mother said in an angry tense tone. She tried to lose Ring by increasing her speed. Ring kept up. Sighing, Mother pulled over and stopped.

"Open the door and let him in!" Mother looked straight ahead without speaking.

As soon as the car door opened, Ring jumped in the back seat and sat like a canine king. A panting king. I was relieved that Ring was safe now; he wouldn't get run over.

After Mother dropped me off at school, she returned home with Ring.

When Mother picked me up after school, she said through the open car window,

"Get that dog in the car!"

"What dog, Mother?"

"That dog! Ring! Look behind you!" Behind me stood a contented Ring, and I was sure he was smiling.

Saying, "Hi there, Ring," I opened the car door and Ring jumped in.

"Why did you bring him?" I asked, curious. It was not a good time for curiosity; Mother was really irritated.

"*I didn't bring him.* He was sitting there by the school principal at the school door when I drove up. Ring was watching all the kids leave and did not move until he saw you. He was waiting for you. We have to do something about this dog's chain."

Back at home, we found the gate still latched. I opened it and Ring followed me into the backyard. Ring had ripped the cotton cord apart and – evidently – he had scaled the chain link fence, too. I tied the rope back together, a temporary fix until we came up with another solution.

We bought a thin chain, strong enough to anchor Ring ... until he broke loose again the next day. Ring followed us to school once again until we stopped the car. He finally trained us to take him with us until we could get a stronger leash. After that, Ring was no longer angry, except when strangers came into the yard. Ring figured the meter man was fair game. The heavy tow chain was gone for good. Soon thereafter, when the whitewall tires of the 1953 Olds rolled up the driveway on a return trip from the grocery store, one of the brown grocery bags contained *canned* dog food. It became a part of our family grocery list and Ring's regular diet.

Uncle Vincent on duty, perhaps in England

X

My Mother's Crystal Bowl

I was twelve years old; it was the year of responsibility.

Throughout the neighborhood, neighbors fought the heat as best they could. Some opened windows, hoping for a breeze. Others inserted air conditioners into living room windows. Each family did its best to counter twelve or more hours of Texas sunshine.

My mother was a meat packager at the Minimax store downtown. Trained to a strong work ethic, she worked and earned her way. She demonstrated her discipline by earning enough to buy a home of our own. She was a blue-collar worker, who wore a white collar to match the rest of her uniform.

Mom's biggest work challenge was waking up in the morning. Her wind-up clock lacked a snooze button. Mother improvised. Her oldest child became her snooze button.

"Wake me up in fifteen minutes," she said as she rolled over.

One look at Mother's legs and anyone could see the

mileage logged on meat market concrete floors. Once she was up in the morning, she cooked a hot breakfast to send me off to school, before she went to work. Returning from a long day at the meat market, she would prepare another hot meal for our dinner. Seeing her exhaustion after work and cooking, I decided to make it my responsibility to clean my mom's house on Saturdays. I determined that she would come home to a clean house.

My new Saturday morning routine began with breakfast. Then, with the radio tuned to my favorite pre-teen radio music, I swept floors, mopped and sometimes waxed. I dusted and sometimes polished furniture. I filled the clothesline with clothes Mother left in a wooden bushel basket. I didn't do laundry, but during the summer months, I did do windows. Dancing under the lawn sprinkler was such fun on a scorching Texas summer day, having clean windows was only an excuse to play in the water.

The smile on my mother's face when she returned from work Saturday afternoon was all the compensation I needed. Saturday nights when she got paid, we went to our favorite drive-in hamburger place where I ordered a hamburger on a sesame seed bun, French fries and a strawberry milkshake. Saturday nights were a special time for mother and daughter. The aroma of hamburgers sizzling on the grill greeted us as soon as Mother turned the car's ignition off. Our regular order was delivered to our car by a waitress called a car hop. We listened to rock 'n' roll music or the sounds of the latest tunes from the Hit Parade piped throughout the drive-in while eating in our car.

My vocabulary did not include the words "weekly allowance." If those words were in Mother's vocabulary, it was her secret. If I had to define a weekly allowance for me in that time, it was the Saturday night hamburgers. The smell of sizzling hamburgers brings forth those easy going, rewarding moments after a week's work, and that mother-daughter time.

That was the summer I started earning my own money, too. Several of our neighbors were young military wives from northern states who were unaccustomed to our sizzling Texas summers. After a month of sending their washing out to the commercial laundry, and after another month of standing over a steamy ironing board, the young wives were primed for a service I could provide. Hearing the wives' complaints, I decided to set up a summer business. I took in ironing. My fees were reasonable, five cents per article of clothing. It was easy work to earn a nickel ironing a handkerchief and hard work to earn a nickel ironing a United States Army starched fatigue shirt with military creases. The cleaners charged extra for the exacting military creases. Two creases ran down each front side of the shirt and three creases down the back, plus one crease across the back shoulders. The creases were pressed with time-consuming precision. Even to this day, the price of military creases presents a burden to military families. However, at age twelve, all I knew was that I needed to compete with commercial laundries. Seeing my price as a bargain at a nickel a shirt, our neighbors told their neighbors. Soon a civilian neighbor asked me to do her husband's shirts, too. Having learned to iron from my grandmother, who had given me my own little ironing board with a working little girl's iron years before, I was up to the challenge. I learned the military crease by studying a professionally laundered and pressed shirt as an example. It was my "monkey-see, monkey-do" learning. This little monkey was making money!

The money was good until my mother told me to stop because my ironing business was making her electric bill go up. She said something about my "overhead." I didn't understand what she meant. She tried to explain to me about "operating expenses," but that didn't make sense to me either. Finally, she just told me to stop taking in ironing. It was disappointing closing my little business down because I enjoyed doing the ironing – and minding my own little business.

My focus was redirected to other house chores. Mother's living room was decorated in browns and Kelly green. How does a twelve-year-old know *green* from *Kelly green?* I knew it was Kelly green because my mother said so.

"That's Kelly green."

In front of the Kelly green couch was a mahogany coffee table with a smooth, shiny surface. The center of the table was decorated with a heavily starched green-and-white ruffled doily. There in the doily's center was *the bowl*.

The fine crystal bowl looked like a fancy fish bowl to me. It was tinted pink with white flower etchings. It was so pretty. A matching liqueur decanter and small liqueur glasses were all neatly corralled in a wooden tray displayed on a side table. This Mexican glassware was a wedding present to my mother and my biological father. Since I had no memories of him, to me and perhaps to my mother, the only ties that remained of my biological parents' bonding was the wedding gift, the beautiful crystal bowl.

Saturday morning chores came around quickly. I decided to take the room-sized Kelly green rug outside, and drape it on the fence to let sunshine freshen it. Later, I would beat accumulated dust out of the rug. Returning inside, I began to vacuum the floor. The music from my radio was so motivating! Vigorously, I danced with the vacuum to the beat of the music. The vacuum cleaner got stuck on a leg of the coffee table. It was so easy to free it by giving the vacuum cleaner's hose a hardy yank. And so I did. The vacuum cleaner's hose hit the beautiful bowl on the table's smooth mahogany surface and the crystal bowl slid across the table. Desperately, I dropped the hose and lurched to catch the bowl before it fell upon the cement-tiled floor. My body seemed to move in slow motion. The bowl plummeted from the table and crashed on the floor faster than I could ever imagine.

Mom's beautiful pretty pink bowl was shattered into too many pieces to count. My heart was shattered, too. The nursery rhyme sounded in my head,

> *Humpty Dumpty sat on the wall,*
> *Humpty Dumpty had a great fall*
> *... and my mother is going to kill me.*

My eyes instantly locked upon the living room clock. It was almost eleven o'clock in the morning; Mom came home at five-thirty in the evening. My mind racing, I hurried to get the broom. I swept up all the broken pieces. I grouped them together. Then, I ran to the hall closet to get the bottle of amber-colored Stanley home glue.

Luck was on my side. The bowl's circular, fluted rim was only in three pieces. I glued those pieces together pretty quickly. Luck was still on my side because I had experience working with various 500-piece puzzles, which was what the bowl reminded me of. It was time to turn the radio off and begin to refocus on the new project. Beginning with the larger pieces, I began the reassembly.

By mid-afternoon, my eyes were crossed and I was exhausted. Perhaps it was not just mental strain; it may have been the fumes from the glue. Regardless, my head was whirling. A rest on the couch for a few minutes would help. While I rested, my eyes gazed at my hands. A few cuts were apparent on my lightly blood-stained fingers. My wounds were bonded shut with the glue, the same glue that had stung my fingers numb. And probably my brain, too. But my efforts were paying off. The puzzle pieces were coming together to resemble a bowl. I was ahead of the time for three-dimensional puzzles that came years later. Perhaps I was innovative, but the better, most fitting word would be *desperate*. My focus returned to getting my mother's bowl back together again. The white flower etchings weren't as lovely with veins of the amber glue. The bowl was taking on a new style – like what it was – ornamentally fragmented.

When all the attached pieces were in place, there was one piece missing, a half-inch obtuse triangular window on the side of the bowl. I searched for the missing piece to make every part interlock to make the bowl whole again. The missing part was nowhere to be found.

I replaced the now amber-veined bowl in the center of the coffee table on the pretty doily. The glass bowl was staged such that the gaping hole left by the missing piece faced away from the door my mother would enter. Then I sat on the Kelly green couch and waited for Mom to come home from work. My thoughts wandered – or maybe it was the glue – anyway, in my thoughts, I wondered if she would like the bowl again. Or would she feel a terrible sorrow that the lovely wedding gift would never be the same? I stared at the bowl and waited for Mom to come home. I didn't feel like doing any other chores. My motivation and strength were deflated. Silent and remorseful, I sat in the silence of the living room ... and waited. The pain of imagining Mom's disappointment was real. And so was the anticipation of my discipline to come.

The back door flew open, startling me. Mother was home. Finally. Dressed in a white uniform, Mom carried her stained meat market apron and her purse. She saw me sitting on the couch, but she could not see my agonizing heart. Mother's words of wisdom echoed in my mind then, as they sometimes do today. "*Dichos,*" my grandmother might say.

"Honesty is the best policy." The other phrase Mother raised me on was, "if there is a will there is a way." I was compelled to stand up and confess like a good Catholic. The words spilled out from somewhere inside me.

"Mom, I accidently broke your bowl today while I was cleaning." That took care of "honesty is the best policy." Then I continued, "I glued it back together." That took care of the "if there's a will there's a way" wisdom.

Mom walked closer slowly to get a better look at the warped bowl sitting on the green and white starched doily. Mother's jaw dropped ever so slightly; she looked sad, so sad. The bowl just looked plain pitiful. I don't think she even saw the little gapping window on the side of the bowl where the glass piece was missing. Anxiously, I waited through a petrifying silence until she finally spoke.

"You ... you tried to glue it back together?" she asked in disbelief.

"Yes ma'am. There's hardly any glue left. I'm sorry, Mother," I said, overcome by guilt. I had broken the bowl, and furthermore, I had used up most of her glue.

There was another brief silence.

"Just put it in the trash." She said, barely above a whisper. Then she sighed. It was all she did before retreating to her bedroom.

I pulled myself from the couch, still feeling light-headed. My wounded hands reached for the bowl and my wounded heart wished, *if only it had been just a plain glass fish bowl.* I carried the sticky bowl to the garbage can. I buried the misshapen bowl with its amber veins under a tabloid sale circular, just as I had disposed of the collard greens with bacon drippings that I was supposed to have eaten one Sunday the year before. I had buried the collard greens under a newspaper, too, and recalling that only increased my shame. There was very little consolation in the fact that now I had permission to bury the bowl.

My thoughts were interrupted. I was startled when Mother called out.

"Get ready, so we can go eat hamburgers!" Her words released something in me that had been wound tighter than I realized.

My mother's decision not to discipline me made me sigh. As I reflect on that day, I know I learned a few more lessons. Unknown even to me at the time, that bowl served as a premature prototype for the 3-D or globe puzzles that the future had in store for my generation. Now I was set with the experience of putting those puzzles together. In the future, they would be more fun.

I also learned another lesson. Sometimes things can be so broken that there's no glue to make them beautiful anymore, no matter how hard you try. That day I also learned something by example: the beauty of love and forgiveness. It was also a lesson realized from one of my *abuelita*'s dichos – "*En la juventud aprendemos, en la vejez entendemos.*" Yes, *Abuelita* was right – in youth we learn, in old age we understand. My mother loved the beautiful pink bowl with its matching decanter set. But her love for me was expressed in patience, understanding and forgiveness flavored with Saturday night hamburgers. Her unconditional love was more beautiful than any crystal bowl.

XI

An Extra Cup

It was an unexpected kind gesture.

It was hard for me to understand.

Why would she do this?

After my *abuelita's* death, *Tía Jesusita* and her family became my dearest extended family. When I was young, *Tía* invited me to join my cousins for Mexican sweet bread, *pan de dulce* we called it, served with a cup of Ovaltine or Bosco or maybe a cup of Borden's, *leche.* I learned the English word for milk was *Borden's* because that's what was printed on the cartons.

Una taza, a cup meant different things in *Tía's* home too. Sometimes, a cup meant a real cup which was a free prize found inside a detergent box, a marketing practice of those times, or a simple patterned glass, which had come into the house a few weeks before full of grape jelly. There was always room at *Tía's* kitchen table for a visiting cousin; there was always room for an extra cup. Sometimes on a cold winter morning, when she grabbed the wooden carved handle with attached chocolate-stained wooden-carved blades, we knew we were in for a delicious treat. She used her Mexican wooden beater and whipped up some delicious Mexican hot chocolate with *canela*, the Mexican cinnamon spice. The aromatic blend of the Mexican chocolate with cinnamon lingered in her kitchen. The liquid blend of the spiced chocolate kept us warm for the rest of the Texas winter day.

Demonstrations of love and admiration between us were mainly nonverbal in those days. Hugs and other gestures were the affirmations of affection I knew as a young girl. The traditional hug greeting was shared between family members. Preparing to go out one evening when we were teenagers, my cousins went to kiss *Tia* goodbye and to receive her mother's traditional blessing. I stood aside, like the visiting cousin that I was, and watched my cousins approach her one by one. When they were done, and in spite of all my shyness, I found myself going up to *Tia*, too. I hugged her and kissed her check, feeling like I was one of her own. We both chuckled.

The day came when a cousin called to notify me that *Tia Jesusita* was gravely ill. She was so ill when she was taken to the hospital that she was immediately admitted. Being of sound mind, she decided to decline surgery. At eighty-one years of age, her heart was functioning at ten percent of normal capability. Being raised in a loving, generous family, it was difficult to comprehend anyone functioning at ten percent of their heart's capability, especially my vibrant *Tia*. She was on life support, so I made my journey to visit her one last time.

Entering the hospital, I decided to buy her flowers at the florist in the lobby before finding her room. *Tia* loved growing flowers and designing her rock garden vignettes. Normally, my flower selection for hospital visits was a bouquet of various colorful flowers and greenery. This time something compelled me to select a bouquet exclusively of her favorite pink Veronica flowers for my *Tia Jesusita, un ramo de rosas para mi tía* in her delicate condition.

She was in the intensive care unit. I entered quietly, holding the bouquet of flowers before me. *Tia Jesusita* lay very still, her eyes closed. My cousin Lauren had arrived from Washington, D.C., and was by her mother's side. Lauren smiled when she recognized me. Years had passed since we had last seen each other. Lauren spoke quietly, almost whispering.

"Mother, Connie is here."

Tia opened her big, beautiful dark brown eyes and nodded groggily. Her mouth was covered by a medical mask. She was unable to speak.

"Hi *Tia*, I brought you flowers." I smiled at my kind-hearted aunt. Suddenly, alarming things started happening. The machine's digital numerals fluctuated rapidly, which seemed to register that something was out of control.

"Lauren, what is happening?" I asked, alarmed for my aunt.

"I don't know," Lauren said. Neither Lauren nor I were versed in medical ways, but Lauren started calming my aunt down.

Confusion added to my alarm, and I said, "Maybe I should leave. I'll be back later." I feared that I might have done something wrong. Perhaps *Tia* only wanted immediate family there. I reasoned that my place was to go join other family members in the waiting room. My cousin Mia met me in the waiting room. She saw me walk in with the flowers. We hugged each other. I nervously explained how my visit with *Tía* had not gone well. Something had happened and Lauren was tending to *Tía*.

Mia, a registered nurse, left immediately to see what was happening. It was only natural in more ways than one. Remaining in the waiting room, I sat with the bouquet of lovely flowers in my arm, worrying that I had upset my aunt's fragile health. Fear overwhelmed me: had I done something to trigger this life-threatening episode?

Mia returned later to report her mother was okay. I asked if it was something I had done. Mia explained, "No, no, she just got excited." Mia's explanation was not clinical to me, calm but not clinical.

"But, why?" I asked. "Mia, I just walked in and told her I had brought her flowers, that's all." I tried to explain in an apologetic manner. At the same time, I showed Mia the flowers.

"Connie, Mother loves flowers," Mia said quietly.

I continued to explain and apologize. "Why do you think she got excited? Did I do something ... wrong? I didn't mean to cause her discomfort."

"I don't know, Connie," Mia continued. "Here, I'll take them and save them for her. Flowers are not allowed in the ICU, anyway."

Later that day, I went to visit *mi Tía* once again. This time, it was okay. She took off her mask and mumbled softly asking about the *flores*. I let her know the flowers had to remain outside because the people who decide such things in hospitals didn't allow flowers in her room.

"*Locos.*" She mumbled barely above a whisper. She called

them "crazy ones." For the first time, I realized how much she loved the color pink in flowers. They were all around her yard. The clues were there, *mi Tia* named her youngest daughter after the pink color of the Veronica flower. *Tia* wore a lovely rosy pink-colored dress in her portrait. Her daughters were wearing rosy pink dresses in their portraits.

I kissed her forehead and touched her aged bronze hand. Her two long braids rested on her collar bones. Big dark brown eyes with long black lashes opened below the natural arch of her eyebrows. Remembering how she used to comb her hair as my grandmother had, in two braids entwined on top of her head in a crowning style, my thoughts rambled. *Tia* was the last of her generation to wear her long braids in the old Mexican female custom. Who would continue the tradition now? Sometimes *Tia Jesusita* wore her hair in a bun on the back of her head, as she did on the day of the kind gesture several years before her illness.

Again my hand touched hers as I reminisced.

Long ago on that day of the kind gesture, I was taking my leave after a visit with her. On that day, she said, "*Espera*." She wanted me to wait. She disappeared into her kitchen and returned to the back room where I waited. Returning, she opened a cabinet where she stored her dishes, opened the cabinet and reached for a creamer on the top shelf. Cupping the creamer in her remarkably *mestizo* hands, she gave me an apologetic glance, which I failed to understand. Why, I wondered?

We both stared at the creamer in her hands. The creamer was a medium greyish blue from the bottom to the brim, which was a semi-fluorescent golden amber. Where these two colors met a bold black line ran around the creamer. I remembered that there had once been matching cups and saucers. Visions of us cousins, sitting around her kitchen table came to mind. I remembered enjoying the warmth of the hot Mexican chocolate *Tia* served us in the matching cups.

Gazing at me again as if an apology was due, she finally smiled and spoke. "I had three cups. This is left from my serving set." She paused and lifted the creamer to me. "I gave the girls each a cup. I have no more cups left, but I saved this for you. I wanted to be sure you got it." *Tia Jesusita* presented the creamer to me.

I accepted the creamer, the precious sentimental heirloom, a prize that originally came straight from a detergent box and now came straight from her generous heart. The gift was so unexpected. We hugged. I assured her the creamer would have an honored place in my small collection of creamers. *No lo sabía,* she didn't know of my creamer collection until that day. I added another creamer in my favorite color of blue from my loving aunt to my collection.

My eyes blinked away the memory of that day; that was then and this was now, a sad new day. It was time for me to go. I let her soft hand rest on the hospital bed that also held her sensitive loving heart.

At what time in our lives do we understand everything? Or why some things happen?

There is never a need to apologize for what we give to one another, especially when we express our love in the giving. In my aunt's home, there were different definitions of a cup: mugs used for serving hot Mexican chocolate with *canela,* tea cups with saucers, and bonus tumblers that were actually glasses in which she served Borden's milk. There were cups for serving coffee to visiting guests, "cups" of tall glass for drinking cold ice tea blended with sun-ripened yellow lemons, or perhaps citrus yellow lemonade, limeade or Kool-Aid (also with lemons). *Mi Tia's* were cups of family love, *éstas eran tazas de amor de la familia.* Sometimes, the cups were served with a little sweetness from Ovaltine or Bosco; but always her cups were served with love from the heart. In my aunt's home, there was the loving, giving spirit of aging bronze *mestizo* hands and a delicate sensitive heart. There was always room for one more at her serving table, always an extra cup.

XII

Getting Smarter Than a Fifth-Grader

In first grade, I overheard my teacher whisper to another, saying I was *slow*. In the second grade, and again in the third grade, I heard it again. When was I going to get faster and *smarter* than a fifth-grader? Eventually, I found myself in the sixth grade. Surely, by now I must be smarter than a fifth-grader!

That was the year I became aware that grades were a reflection and a measurement of a student's intelligence. It became evident to me that perhaps the teachers were right.

In sixth grade, I also overheard kids mentioning names of our "smart" classmates. They did not include my name. For the sake of this story, their names were Faith, Hope and Charity. Funny, it was often girls' names rather than boys' names that they whispered. The key thing I never overheard was where or how to enhance one's smartness. The thought crossed my inquisitive mind, and I went to the dictionary, which had become my best friend, explaining things to me in

English or any language. My other best friends turned out to be the library and encyclopedias. I looked up the word "smart" in the dictionary and gave it some serious thought.

Hmmm.

Being smart was a good thing back in the 1950s, and it still is. Over time, I've learned that smartness comes in many different ways. And it comes at different stages of life. At the time, the realization occurred to me that perhaps you can get smart eating Smarties candy wafers. In honor of education and my sweet tooth, I had to try. A friend advised me that neither candy nor any amount of study would affect my Intelligence Quotient (IQ). Like a sweet tooth, she said, I had inherited my IQ.

I thought, *well it's a good thing something can be done about bad manners!*

Over the decades, studies do show ways (other than eating candy with "smart" in the name) to increase a person's IQ – or at least one's test scores. Even in the sixth grade, I learned that being smart had nothing to do with being citizen of the week.

Charity, Faith, Hope and I were in Brownies and then Girl Scouts together. Charity became my best friend in sixth grade. Charity explained what a diary was when I received one for my birthday. She encouraged me to write in it every day.

Faith's mother hosted scout troop meetings at her house. Mrs. Brunson served cookies and pink lemonade. P-i-n-k, *pink* lemonade! I was a little afraid to drink it because I had never seen pink lemons. Curiosity (and my sweet tooth) won out. I had to try just a little. My grandmother had instructed me that, when I was a guest in someone's home, I must at least try the food I was given regardless of how strange the food appeared. *Una prevadita*, I was to take "only a little taste." Eureka! I had two servings! It was so good, tasty and refreshing. I told my mother about the beverage adventure. Soon, she started serving pink lemonade, too.

But it was Hope who was the most influential of the three. Hope was a blonde-haired, blue-eyed friend who wore glasses, like me. She was a little taller than me and had straight teeth. She was really smart. I thought I could learn something from her. She sat across the aisle from me, our desks parallel to each other.

My first observation of Hope was that *she took her books home every day*. I did, too, but in my case, it was to complete the homework others had finished during class time. I only read to write the answers down. But one day I realized something new. When our teacher, Mrs. Riemenschneider, asked the class questions, Hope had the right answers. I was curious why. Finally, I heard Mrs. Riemenschneider ask the key question.

"How many of you read the *whole* chapter, last night?"

Many students raised their hands, including all the "smart" kids. They had *read ... the ... whole ... chapter*. The words reverberated in my head. Reading the entire chapter was a strategy I had not really considered before. Most of the time, my homework answers were correct ... probably because I read only to seek the answers. So I began reading to understand and not just looking for words to fill in the blanks on my worksheets. When I began to understand, words began to carry more weight. The weight was comprehension. It was different than words that carried only sounds – blah, blah, blah – to me.

From then on, I decided to study a little harder. For

the poetry recital, the smart kids chose a poem with a higher degree of difficulty from the options the rest of us were given. I do not recall the titles of their poems. I decided to recite, "All Thing Bright and Beautiful" by Cecil Frances Alexander. It was a medium-level degree of difficulty poem, according to the teacher's list. Choosing it was also the first smart thing I did; I realized my limits.

Another thing I noticed about Hope was that she replaced the standard pink block eraser with a white rectangular eraser that she brought from home. The white eraser had a place of honor on the upper right hand corner of her desk, where it displaced the pink eraser that once occupied that spot. I observed her using the white eraser on her school work. I figured it helped Hope be a better student, to be smart.

At home, I talked to my mother. "Mother, I have a friend in school. *She is really smart*; her name is Hope. Hope has a white eraser that she uses for her school work and I think it helps Hope become smart. Mother, maybe if I had a white eraser I could make better grades and become smart. Will you buy me a white eraser to help me get smart?" I supposed having two white erasers would get me smarter and faster twice as quickly, but at that time I lacked the courage to ask for two white erasers. Besides, I knew my learning came slowly.

Mother did buy me a white eraser. I proudly took the white eraser to school and placed it on the upper right hand corner of my desk just like Hope did. At first, I tried erasing every time Hope did. But exactly why and where the erasing was to take place was not clear to me. It occurred to me it was an eraser to use only when you made penmanship writing mistakes or when writing down wrong answers. Unfortunately, the correct answers for homework did not come as easily or as quickly for me as they did for Hope. My white eraser was used more often and soon became a non-scholastic shade of gray. Of course, my white block eraser also became a stub rather quickly, too.

Another observation struck me about the "smart" ones: they wore something called petticoats or crinolines under their skirts. A quick session with the dictionary informed me that petticoats were not really coats or overcoats. These petticoats were *under* coats, actually *under* skirts featuring tiers of ruffles. They were often made of stiffly starched nylon netting. Petticoats made skirts puff out. I didn't know why skirts had to puff out so; but it seemed a requirement of smartness. Naturally, the more crinolines the girls wore, the more puffed out their skirts appeared.

Hope came to school wearing petticoats under a new skirt. The skirt looked so full it looked like a wide umbrella hanging from Hope's small waist. She had to push down on her skirt with both hands to get down the aisle just to reach her desk. When she sat down, the petticoat, skirt and all, swirled. Once Hope and her skirt settled in her desk, I saw the dog on her skirt. It was a black poodle dog. Her dressing style made her look smart, too. In future dialogue, some would have said "she had it going on."

When Mother came home from work, we talked. I mentioned to Mother how Hope had come to school wearing a poodle skirt and it made her smart and even made Hope look smart.

"Mother ...," I said breathlessly, "if I had a skirt with a poodle on it, it might help me become smart, too. Do you think you could find one for me?"

Mother said she would try to find one for me. A few days later, mother came home with a brown paper bag filled to the top with clothes. I was familiar with such bags of clothes that were given to my mother by her friend whose daughter had outgrown them. The daughter and I were the same age and school grade. My slower growth rate made her hand-me-downs just about perfect.

The paper bag was always a welcome sight. I took it to my room and spread the hand-me-downs out on my bed. I separated out those that I, also, had already outgrown. At the very bottom of the bag, I found a pretty Kelley green wool skirt that was adorable. Pulling it out enthusiastically, I slipped it on. It fit fine. There was one skirt left in the bag, a gray wool skirt which, when I held it up to my waist, I found to have a black woolly poodle embroidered near the hem. The wool puffed out from the gray skirt, making the dog's fur look real. A pink ribbon accented the poodle's neck.

Finally I had a poodle skirt!

Surely, wearing a poodle skit (just like Hope) would help me get smart (and look smart)!

Mother took the skirt to the commercial cleaners. Finally I could wear the skirt to school. I loved the skirt *sooooo much!* The skirt looked mighty fine, though I had only one petticoat.

It was my turn to look like an umbrella! If my skirt puffed out as much as Hope's skirts, I would have no room to move in my seat. People trying to walk down my aisle would have to detour. I wore the poodle skirt to school pretty often, so often that the woolly part of the poodle began to fray. The poor dog developed a bad case of mange.

At the end of sixth grade, I decided that my classmates and I all learned at different rates, in different ways and at different times. I decided that erasers, beverages and clothing were important for their respective uses, but probably did not materially affect a person's smarts. I came to realize that the chapters read in books likely had the most effect on making anyone smarter than a fifth-grader. I concluded that the only smart thing for me to do was to stop wearing the skirt with the poor mangy poodle. And I did.

XIII

El Milagro del Corazon

The Miracle of the Heart

After *Doña Basilia*'s sister's death at a young age, *Doña Basilia* felt a responsibility to her sister's children, who came to her when they needed a little extra nurturing, support or advice. Eventually, all the children married except the youngest son, Carlos.

At last Carlos came to live with his aunt, *Doña Basilia*, who he later called "Mama." I knew him as *Tio* Carlos; some of my cousins called him Carlos, other cousins lovingly called him *Tio Toto*. *Tio* is the Spanish word for uncle while *Tia* is the word for aunt.

It seemed to me *Tio* Carlos had lived with my grandmother since I was born. Much older than me, he was of medium height (among Mexican-American men) with light brown-sugar-colored skin and thick black hair. His dark brown eyes were framed between a square jaw and black, bushy eyebrows. Carlos left my grandmother's house every day to work in blue overalls with gray thin stripes, a heavy cotton sky-blue shirt and a railroad man's cap. A jovial conversationalist, Carlos was always good-natured. I can't recall him ever being angry. Once, I think he pretended to be angry. When he could sustain the ruse no longer, his hearty belly laugh gave him away. When not laughing, Carlos was calm and secure. He laughed harder and louder at me than anyone I ever knew.

Sometimes *Tio* extended his hand out to me and said, "*Cómo estás,* How are you?" It was his greeting for "How are you?" Funny, I never realized it, but he was bilingual. He could read, write and speak Spanish and English.

My hand extended up to meet this big, rugged manly hand. He would grasp my hand and shake, shake, shake my hand for what seemed forever. Eventually I began to laugh and giggle until he let go of my hand. Then his belly laugh, whole-hearted and affectionate, seemed to shake everything in the room. I fell for his handshake trick all the time – even as adults neither one of us outgrew our greeting.

He was a forty-six-year-old bachelor. I never knew him to go drinking or dancing. Bachelorhood seemed to suit him. He never dated. Now and then he enjoyed going to the movies, *a las películas.* My guess, he went to the Alameda in downtown San Antonio.

After his Saturday night bath, he shaved in his bedroom. I'd watch him shave in his bedroom as he prepared to go to, as he said, *al cho.* Often, I would stand by his dresser as *Tio* Carlos began his ritual. I was fascinated at how he made magic with his shaving cup and brush. I waited outside his bedroom, same as the one where I was born. His mule chest of drawers was right next to his bedroom entry. Sometimes while I waited outside, I rolled my hand into a fist on one hand and then on the other trying to decide which hand was the best knocking fist. Listening intently until I heard him opening and closing drawers or rattling things on the chest, I slid my shoes, sandals or bare feet under the curtain that was a make-do door. When he heard my tap, tap, tap on the door frame, he would ask, "*¿Quién es?*"

I wondered why he had to ask "who is it?" Surely he could see my feet or shoes. Pushing my feet further underneath the curtain, I knocked again. Tap, tap, tap.

"*¿Quién es?*" he asked again.

"*Soy yo. Mire mis pies.*" Surely, he must know that it was me. "Look at my feet." "Okay," was his key note of entry. But, other times, he'd say, "*No conozco los pies.*" How could he not know my feet, we did this so often? Then he gave his "okay."

I pulled the curtain aside and placed myself right next to his chest of drawers.

During the day, while he was at work, I sneaked a peek into his shaving cup looking for the cup's magic; it was always empty. Yet, once a week, right after his Saturday night bath, he made magic with his shaving cup. His wand was the soft-bristled shaving brush. A little blessing of water and a brisk rotation of the wrist – and he created magic foam in his shaving cup. Sometimes, he hummed as he pulled up his brush with foamy peaks. *Tío* looked as if he was about to eat an ice cream cone. Like an artist at work, he and the shaving brush painted a foamy white beard on his bronze face until he looked just like a Mexican Santa Claus.

Once in a while, he tapped my glistening nose with the scented foam as I watched in awe. The performance continued. With a delicate touch, his man-sized hand carried the steel-edged razor in a gliding motion down his brown-sugar pigmented, fuzzy wuzzy cheek. Next, he repeated the motion above his lips, over his chin and onto his other cheek, all the while using his free hand to pull his facial "canvas" taunt. Occasionally, he dipped the silver razor into a bowl of water to remove the magic foam. I was a child in awe watching him shave. Unlike my youngest uncle, Henry, *Tio* Carlos very, very rarely had pieces of toilet paper with red dots plastered to his face. The final touch was a sprinkle on his hands from an old cream-colored bottle with a ship on it. Ahhhh, the scent of a man, as I remember from my childhood.

After his shaving ritual, and realizing it was time for him to leave for the Saturday night movies, I ran to the front screen door to watch him walk away from *Abuelita's* home. Most often, I stood at the front screen door to say, "*Adiós, Tio*" to bid him goodbye. He continued walking down the inclined driveway. Without turning around, he waved his macho hand from side to side in the air and said, "Bye," probably smiling, although I could not see his face. It was our Saturday night custom ... until the night years later when his departure changed.

On this night, right after I bid him "goodbye" as he walked down the driveway, he did a special little skip and hop. At first, I thought he had stumbled on a rock. Then I noticed that his steps were noticeably lively and he was swinging his arms sprightly. This became *Tio's* new habit. In today's slang, he had *swag goin' ooooon*. It was very comical to me; quite naturally, I thought he was trying to make me laugh – and he did.

During a visit when I began seventh grade, *mi abuelita* called me into the kitchen to help her. In the evenings, as the sun was setting behind the big mesquite in the backyard, *Abuelita* and I sat at her kitchen table, the one with the faux marble top and chrome legs. There, we began our sunset task: shelling pecans. We removed the pecan halves from hard shells and placed them in a bowl. However, I popped some kernels into my mouth. It was okay to feed the help. We always carefully removed the bark-like, heart-shaped piece found in between the two pecan halves. That piece of the pecan tastes bitter, very bitter.

My grandmother called this *el corazón de la nuez*, the heart of the pecan. She collected *los corazones de las nueces* until there was a small mound, just enough to make tea. Sliding one hand over the table, she gathered the hearts in her cupped hand. Water was boiling in a saucepan; there she released the hearts to brew a tea. Pouring the brew into a tea cup and, adding a little sweet – honey or sugar – *miel o azúcar*, she calmly called my uncle into the kitchen.

"Carlos, *su té está listo*," she told him, "Carlos, your tea is ready."

Tío Carlos picked up his cup, sipped from it and then took the tea to his room. I never knew what his ailment was, if any. But I knew of my grandmother's faith healing. I saw the *curandera* in her was at work. On a summer evening, my grandmother and I sat shelling pecans for the tea. *Tío* Carlos walked into the kitchen, stood boldly and made an announcement.

"*Me voy a casar.*" *Tío* Carlos stood boldly and announced, "I am going to get married."

My grandmother stared at him with her mouth partially open in total surprise. He gave his *Tio* Carlos boyish grin. Thank goodness, *mi abuelita* was sitting down when she got the news. I looked at her, then looked at him, then looked at her, then looked again to him. Oh yes, the Felix-the-cat look-see. I had not outgrown it.

I was concerned for both of them. *Casar* meant to marry. I was old enough to know getting married meant moving away from home (at least it did back then). I *was* concerned for both of them.

He married at the age of forty-seven. My grandmother was happy to see her nearly "*Quincuagésimo*" get married. She called him "*Quincuagésimo*" meaning fiftieth, in his case near his fiftieth birthday. She was afraid one day he would be all alone. Beyond the age of reasoning, I realized that his lively steps as he left to go to the movies were all about someone new in his life.

Many years later when he was in his eighties, he became ill and was hospitalized. I was notified and went to visit him. He looked happy, optimistic as always. A big smile grew upon his bronze face when I walked in his room. It was so much like him. We visited for a while. I asked if he needed anything, and he humbly said he was fine. He asked about my family. We visited a while longer before I told him I had written a story about him.

"*¡Sobre mí!*" In his surprise, he exclaimed, "About me!"

I asked him to read it and let me know where my memory had failed me or what he wanted to correct or change.

I gave him the story pages.

Tio took the pages and laid them upon his lap. He reached over to the hospital nightstand for his glasses, unfolded them, then picked up the typed pages and began reading, as if he was handling a newspaper. Able to read and speak both English and Spanish, he held his head still as his large russet-brown eyes moved across each line, digesting every word. Occasionally, he stopped and his eyes blinked rapidly. Then he continued. Flipping each page gently with the tips of his manly fingers, as if each page was a delicate newspaper page, he continued intently.

Once he took a deep breath and held it a moment, as if absorbing a memory, then released his breath along with the memory. Another time he sighed quietly. Finally, he finished reading, assembled the pages in order and handed me the story, *his story*. A satisfied smile spread across his old face.

"What would you like for me to change in the story? Anything?" I asked out of respect for him.

He answered, *"Nada, no cambie nada, está bien como es."* He had given his approval when he said, "Nothing, change nothing, it is good as it is."

I asked *Tio* permission to ask a personal question. He said, "Yes, go ahead and ask."

"After all those years by yourself, why did you wait until you were forty-seven to marry?"

"Ya, estaba maduro para la cosecha." He said. "I was ripe for the picking [harvest]."

He married Goya, a woman who was always smiling. I was given one of their wedding pictures in color, by way of my grandmother, no less. Carlos and Goya had two daughters and several grandchildren. He was a construction laborer until he retired. Then he devoted his time tending his yard and propagating breathtaking roses. One of his daughters mentioned she, too, was captivated with his shaving ritual. *Tío* and his bride remained married until she died. Now, they are buried together.

In later years, I wondered if *Tío* Carlos suffered from a broken heart when he was a young man. Sometimes a broken heart makes a man a bachelor for a long time. Broken hearts taste bitter; they taste like *los corazones de las nueces,* the hearts of the pecans.

I was lucky to have had him in my life to entertain me with his own performing art, shaving. He was lucky to have *Doña Basilia* to call "Mama." He was lucky she was a *curandera,* a faith healer having her good magic to create *el milagro del corazón,* the miracle of the heart.

Reading Group Extras

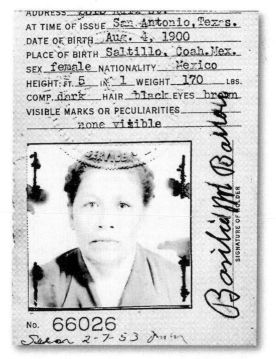

Immigration papers of the author's grandmother, Basilia
Montez Barron, recorded at the Mexican Consulate in
San Antonio, Texas and dated February 7, 1953.

Author Biography

Consuelo Samarripa is a second-generation Texas native, born in the west side *barrios* of San Antonio. She has lived in Killeen and other large and small Texas towns, in Germany, and on Oahu Island in Hawaii. She has traveled in Europe, Canada, Mexico and the United States. She earned her B.S. degree in Computer Science, with graduate studies in Management Science.

An employer advised her to improve on her speaking skills because she was very shy. She joined Toastmasters International educational programs in leadership and communication, where she earned the Distinguished Toastmaster (DTM). At that time, she was among the five percent of Toastmasters who were DTMs in the world. Named Outstanding Toastmaster of the Year in her District, she was one of seventy-five so honored worldwide. During her district-level leadership roles, she attained the World Headquarters recognition with an Excellence in Marketing and an Excellence in Education and Training. After learning of her Toastmasters achievements, the Lone Star Girl Scout Council created the Consuelo Samarripa Leadership Award.

In the University of Texas School of Public Affairs leadership program "Innovation 88," she earned four of five possible recognitions. In researching, developing and writing speeches, Samarripa discovered that her calling was in storytelling.

Developing oral storytelling was a challenge to her. It was much too powerful for her comfort. After attending storytelling conferences and workshops, Consuelo began storytelling professionally in 1996. She was selected to the Texas Commission on the Arts Touring Roster in 2000 after an audience member encouraged her to apply. A founding organizer of the first Tejas Hispanic Storytelling Festival, she produced and directed the festival at Mexic Arte Museum in Austin for seven years.

Consuelo auditioned and was selected for the role of Lone Woman, one of the five leading roles in the play, "Star of the Hills," produced by Emily Ann Theatre (Wimberley, Texas). She wrote and performed the story titled "Just Like Any Kid," a special selection by the Frontera Fest Stage Crew for a repeat performance in "Best of the Fest" week at Hyde Park Theatre (Austin, Texas). Afterward, she played the lead role of "Senora Tortuga" in a touring play production by Teatro Humanidad (Austin, Texas).

Samarripa's historical interpretive story titled "The Passage of Scotland's Four" was selected for publication in the Texas Folklore Society's 2007 anthology, *Folklore in Motion, Texas Travel Lore.*

Consuelo shares her Mexican-American heritage through history, folklore, personal stories, poetry, myths and multicultural tales. Her repertoire also includes ghost stories as well as sacred stories. Unique bilingual blends and "noise makers," as well as her use of shawls, adds interest to her storytelling "Consuelo style." Consuelo's programs entertain audiences in English, Spanish and her own bilingual blends.

Consuelo has three adult children and eight grandchildren.

The author's high school graduation photograph, 1966.
"We did not wear make-up in high school, not until college."

On the left, the author's uncle Vincent, in his US Army dress uniform before deployment to European bases. On the right, The military funeral of Uncle Vincent that was held at Christ the King Church in San Antonio.

U.S. Army honor guard leaving Max Martinez Funeral Home
with Uncle Vincent's body

Author Essay

In some religions, a child reaches the "age of reason" at seven years of age. I recall sounding out words at that age and calling it reading. Months later, I realized that calling out words was not reading, but just sounding out words correctly. That was the first step on my path to reading English as a Spanish-speaking kid. My first books included reading about Jane, Dick and Spot. I even learned Spot had his own language. Most of the time, his language was "Bow-wow!"

There were no bilingual in the schools when I started first grade in Texas. I learned English by what we today call "total immersion" in the big city of San Antonio, Texas, the small town of Killeen, Texas, and in Schwäbisch Gmünd, Germany, where my family lived during my dad's military assignment there. It was years before I read in English to comprehend. Reading exercises helped me remember enough to pass tests; but, it was reading and re-reading that taught me to understand. When that came together for me, I progressed beyond reading textbooks. Reading books for enjoyment allowed me to experience the world through stories in my own room. The meaning of a pretend world (fiction) and the true or real world (nonfiction) only then became apparent. For enjoyment, I read biographies of Abraham Lincoln, Benjamin Franklin, Madame Curie, Booker T. Washington and George Washington Carver, fascinated by their life experiences.

Reading about Benjamin Franklin's experiments inspired me to do an experiment for the Science Fair. I thought up an experiment by first reading a book about experiments to find one that satisfied my curiosity. Honestly, I did not realize the actual meaning of a science fair; I simply knew that something called a science project was required of me. I didn't like to do things by myself, so I asked a really nice girl, Sue Smale, to join me in the project. Our project included a cardboard box, a flashlight that I borrowed from my mother's gadget drawer, one of mother's clear jelly glasses and milk. We set up the experiment in our school room along with the other students' science projects. The day after classroom displays ended, my teacher, Mrs. Riemenschneider, called me to her desk. She looked sad.

"I'm sorry Connie, but the glass of milk spilled when your exhibit was being loaded for the science fair. The box was soaked as your experiment was loaded." She said it in such a regretful tone. Images of a warped cardboard box with a soured milk scent triggered my question.

"Did the glass break?" I was worried that my mother's jelly glass might be broken. Mrs. Riemenschneider assured me the glass was not broken. I sighed, willing the whole project and its gloomy outcome into the past. I certainly was not going to cry over spilled milk when I did not know what consequences might come of it. Days later, Mrs. Riemenschneider announced to the class that Sue and I had won a second-place ribbon in our category. It was a red ribbon with gold lettering. I heard myself gasp as my jaw dropped open. Wow! Later that day, when my inquiring mind had formed the question that had been brewing there, I asked Mrs. Riemenschneider, "Since the milk was spilled, how could we win? It was needed to prove our experiment."

She smiled. "The Science Fair was held at another school. A teacher there found some milk for your experiment." She continued smiling. Accepting her mood, I was vaguely happy, too. Yet I could not escape wondering whether all those who saw our science project suspected that Sue and I weren't quite as scientific as we pretended to be.

The year of the Science Fair project, my friend Cynthia Wren gave me a diary for my birthday, explaining, "You must write in it every day." When I moved away, she was the one who said, "You write." We exchanged letters until boy crushes got in the way.

The next year, I tried another experiments, the effects of gibberellic acid on tomato plants. The school offered the acid and my teacher offered the tomato plant seedlings from her garden. The experiment on the effects of light and darkness on the growth of tomato plants required tracking, which meant I was constantly running from our living room window to a dark attic closet. My next experiment was the effects of gibberellic acid on tomato plants in the light and darkness. The outcomes of the latter experiments were not significant enough to worry my parents, who were relieved when I ceased running into dark attic closets with a flashlight.

My learning went from a personal scientific era to a personal literary era when my family lived in beautiful Germany during parts of my adventurous junior high and high school years. Asked by my freshman English teacher to write about "the most unforgettable character I ever met," I wrote a story about my mother. Miss Jorgensen liked it and encouraged me to continue writing. She gave the class a list of books to read to prepare us for college. Our apartment had no television, so I read Thomas Hardy and Ernest Hemingway from the list. Reading them made me want to find other books and other authors. I also did a little writing. My inspiration came from a Ludwigsburg High School classmate and friend. Bashful and reclusive, I spoke only to a few people. One classmate seemed equally introverted. She, however, shared some of her writing in class. In awe of her courage to share, I was also impressed with her talent for putting words together. Her sentences were eloquent. That day, Beth Hoff and I walked out of class chatting. Recently, I discovered that she is now a best-selling author, writing under the name Elizabeth Berg. Strange as it seems, one of the first stories I retold as a storyteller was a Christmas story from a magazine. Although at the time I did not realize it, the story was written by Elizabeth Berg, who I once knew as my inspiring classmate, Beth Hoff.

Practicing my flute, during those teen years when we lived in Germany, I remember hearing the muffled voices of our landlords' grandchildren laughing in the apartment below. When I resumed playing, the children's laughter began anew. Their most audible laughter came when I tried to hit high C on my scales. They also laughed when I played songs that lacked a flute melody, so that my notes seemed random. Hearing only the notes assigned to my instrument, my downstairs critics had no clue to the whole melody. Of course, in band, other instruments would complete the melody. What would Mama Steinle's grandchildren know about Zacatecas, a Mexican patriotic march? For sure, I did not have the music for the flute solo. Even if I had a complete score, my playing would not impress a foreign audience. I was on my own. When the German children and I finally became friends, they wanted to see my flute. I let each of them try to play it. They giggled, speaking German as the flute was passed from one to the next, like a peace pipe.

Learning a new language also challenged my assimilating nature. Even Elvis Presley had sung in German; language was "cool." Learning and speaking German allowed me to translate for my parents with our landlords and with those we met when we toured along the German border. It also allowed me to join a German Girl Scout troop. They invited me to their meetings where they laughed at my Mexican-accented German. We had fun as they learned English with a Mexican accent, too. There was lots of giggling and laughter. Serious at Christmas, they taught me to sing Silent Night in German. We hugged each other good night when we parted after meetings. I watched in amazement as they trimmed a Christmas tree in the old tradition: adorning a real tree with three-inch candles which, when lit, glowed through the angel hair with a platinum aura that seemed truly heavenly. Their proud respect of sacred culture, in spite of the WWII aftermath, impressed upon me the importance of preserving my Mexican-American culture. I remained friends with a few German scouts after we returned to the United States. Learning their culture helped me understand my own.

Back in Texas at age seventeen, I was sheltered in traditional Mexican culture. Going away to college was out of the question. Instead, I got a job as a bus girl in our town's newest, grandest hotel, the Cowhouse Hotel. My parents drove me to work sometimes, other times I got a taxi because I did not know how to drive. I saved enough money to enroll at a local night business school, walking to classes after work. My parents picked me up at ten o'clock. The counselor enrolled me in computer languages, which launched my career later. Another lucky break had come my way as the first female of my culture to earn a degree in computer science at Central Texas College. English class did not go as well. The challenge of my freshman English professor, Donna Ingham, resulted in a determination to learn how to write. Her assignments forced me to experiment with writing. The seed she planted matured through hard work and experimentation.

Later, I carpooled with friends to junior college. Then I took a driver's education class, earning my license at age twenty-one.

The Vietnam War interrupted my marriage when my husband enlisted. His tour of duty in Hawaii ended as we returned stateside with three babies under three. My husband and I juggled college classes and parenting when we returned to Killeen continuing our education at Central Texas College. We scheduled our classes so that I stayed home with the babies while he attended classes, then I met him at the campus Bell Tower with my carload of babies. Even our toddlers learned our routine, as became apparent when they asked, "We go to kool?"

My toddlers fed the ducks in the Bell Tower pond when we arrived early. My husband and I switched cars and it was my turn to attend classes. Once, a business law professor allowed me to attend a class with my little daughter, Karen. Otherwise, I would have had to miss his class that day. He gave his permission with the caveat that we would have to leave the class if Karen misbehaved. I assured him that Karen would behave and that I would leave with her if necessary. To Karen, I whispered, "Shhh, we go to kool."

Once employed, my professional evaluations reflected my need to learn communication skills. While my business writing was fine, business also involved speaking at meetings. Andy Drott, a peer, encouraged me to join Toastmasters to become a better communicator. Toastmasters was total emersion all over again. Talking to groups of adults was challenging for me, the introvert. After much struggle, I achieved the level of Distinguished Toastmaster before turning to a series in Spanish to attain the level of Able Toastmaster Bronze. Researching my

Wedding of Uncle Carlos Montez Salas and his bride, Gregoria, known as "Goya"

speeches increased my knowledge, vocabulary and my writing.

As an adult I read history and biographies. Recently, I have also enjoyed reading Elizabeth Berg's novels, remembering her as Beth Hoff, my German high school classmate. Now I love attending my grandkids' birthday parties, school and sports activities. It is always a pleasure taking all my grandchildren to dinner and a movie; soon I will need a bus to cart them all. It is delightful when I can read a story that I am developing to my grandchildren; they are a good gauge, just like my daughter and sons have been about some of my story topics.

Sharing my stories allows others to know that we often share similar footsteps and experience. I understand what it is like being with people foreign to my customary ways of life and language. Some people who have migrated to this country do not understand what it was like to be forbidden to speak their native tongue in school. Or to meet the challenges of a school day when there were no tools or no one to help make your way in a new life.

I guess my philosophy agrees with Booker T. Washington who said, "I have learned that success is to be measured not so much by the position that one has reached in life as by the obstacles which he has had to overcome while trying to succeed."

As for me, it has not been so much about the success as it has been the journey itself. The journey was not easy sometimes, but the age-old Mexican saying, "sí, se puede" often kept me moving ahead. The saying means "yes, it can be done." This journey has been a pleasant one for me; I wish pleasant journeys for you, too.

Consuelo

Q & A With Author

Consuelo Samarripa

Q: Why this book?

A: Both writers and authors speak about writing their memoirs, but seldom are those memoirs written. I have often associated memoirs with great movie stars, politicians, diplomats and other such notables. So, I am a little uneasy calling this collection of stories memoirs. These stories are a collection of adventures, events, experiences and characters that were prominent and influenced me in the 1950s and 1960s. It is a reflection of our Mexican-American customs and how we lived in San Antonio, Texas, and beyond. The stories were written on paper, and then stored digitally. Digital storage changes with time, so I kept a hard copy of each story. Now it was time to get the stories published.

Q: Why was it time to get the stories published?

A: I see students who have immigrated to the United States with their families – not only from Latin American countries, but others as well. Canada and England, of course, and others, too, like Europe, Africa, Samoa, the Philippines, Guam, the Middle East, Vietnam and other Asian countries. Perhaps they, too, will document their assimilation to the United States as part of their family history.

Q: What message do you want to leave the reader?

A: There are many messages in a number of different ways.

For my children and their children, these are memories I want to share, even though I don't tell these stories too often. There is a quote I read once that is similar to this: "like fragrances of a blossom, no one knows what becomes of his or her influence." I wanted to write a little family history honoring those who have passed on, tell moments of their story because *it is their story, too.* I also wanted to share clips of history and unknown lore so my children and grandchildren would understand their ancestral roots.

For other children of any age who have thought they are awkward, clumsy, wimpy, quirky or just don't get it – or maybe even some kids who think they're not good enough because they are different or live a life different from what may be "normal" in their generational day – I hope to let them know not to worry. Especially those who have emigrated from other countries. One day everything will come together. Just do not give up on yourself. Unwelcome incidents will happen, but so will friendly, enjoyable, life-rewarding experiences.

For writers, "ditto" what I said for children. Some of us believe there is a child within each of us for a lifetime, and there are stories to share.

Q: What educational value does the book offer?

A: The book compares and contrasts the different lifestyles and social norms in communities in and out of Texas – some of which are so closely the same. This is a point of view from Texas.

Certainly, there is accepting the challenge of moving

toward assimilating in any state or country, which can be more difficult than moving to another city or across town. However, our customs and traditions are carried with us wherever we go. As these stories are shared, there are more people of Mexican heritage expressing their same experiences. At the same time, the generational era of those who share the experiences are diminishing. There is an awareness of diversity issues that is lost in the next and subsequent generations.

Q: How did you get interested in writing?

A: It was a friendly accident. I received a diary for my birthday from a friend. Yet, another friend explained to me what it was and that I must write in it every day. "Just write," she said. I trusted her advice.

Q: Any discoveries in writing the book?

A: Yes, several in many ways. There was the discovery of my written storytelling voice versus my oral storytelling voice. There was my voice discovery at various chronological ages. There was the struggle with the anonymity of some of my relatives and friends. And there was the discovery of how my shyness and compliance with society's boundaries may have been hurtful to others. I hope they understand and forgive me.

Q: Do you have a favorite story in your collection?

A: Wow, each story is like one of my children. Like with my own children, I dearly love them all. When my children became adults and went out into the world, I had to let them go and let the world experience what they offered. I have no favorite story, but parts of each story bring back joyful memories.

Q: Are there any favorite parts in the book?

A: Remembering my grandmother's kitchen, the feeling of relief from her healing me from angst, our interpretations of reading "Henry" and her roses and delphiniums. Others are the Saturday night hamburgers with my mother, shopping for my babies and running into Davy in the store, my Uncle Carlos' shaving and the scent of Old Spice, the moment I received the lovely creamer from my aunt and my first dog, first bicycle and first box of crayons.

Taken in Mexico, this old photo shows the author's grandmother, Basilia Barron (at right) with an elderly relative, Tersa Montez.

Q: Besides short stories, what other genre do you write or publish?

A: Writing poetry has come rather easy for me – rhyming poetry. The poems are mostly spontaneous spoken words – on the fly – and like a butterfly, they fly away with the wind. I also have enjoyed writing speeches and historical papers.

The Texas Folklore Society published my historical interpretive story, "The Passage of Scotland's Four," in its 2007 anthology, "Folklore in Motion, Texas Travel Lore."

Q: How did you find your publisher?

A: Many years ago, I met Ted Parkhurst at a Texas Library Association Conference, which is attended by many librarians, authors and publishers. Ted and I visited about a book in the future. For many years, it was life interrupted for us both. We met again, in early 2013, and we revisited again about a book. Then, publishing the book was in motion.

Q: Had you worked with other publishers before Parkhurst Brothers?

A: Yes, but the historical paper for the anthology was short and merely involved the legalities of publishing. This book was on a larger scale. The whole idea of a book was intimidating to me – a commitment to the publisher that I might not be able to fulfill. But Ted, perhaps unknowingly, immediately eliminated my worries; it has been a much-appreciated experience publishing with Parkhurst Brothers.

Q: What is your next writing project?

A: There are so many on my list. There is a historical paper I began and want to continue researching. I also want to continue researching genealogy, which progresses slower as our elders pass on.